BORDERS.
CLASSICS

EMILY DICKINSON

Selected Poems

BORDERS.
CLASSICS

CONTENTS

LIFE

This is my letter to the world,
   That never wrote to me, –
The simple news that Nature told,
   With tender majesty.

Her message is committed
   To hands I cannot see;
For love of her, sweet countrymen,
   Judge tenderly of me!

Success is counted sweetest
By those who ne'er succeed.
To comprehend a nectar
Requires sorest need.

Not one of all the purple host
Who took the flag today
Can tell the definition,
So clear, of victory,

As he, defeated, dying,
On whose forbidden ear
The distant strains of triumph
Break, agonized and clear.

Soul, wilt thou toss again?
By just such a hazard
Hundreds have lost, indeed,
But tens have won an all.

Angels' breathless ballot
Lingers to record thee;
Imps in eager caucus
Raffle for my soul.

Our lives are Swiss,—
So still, so cool,
Till, some odd afternoon,
The Alps neglect their curtains,
And we look farther on.

Italy stands the other side,
While, like a guard between,
The solemn Alps,
The siren Alps,
Forever intervene!

Within my reach!
I could have touched!
I might have chanced that way!
Soft sauntered through the village,
Sauntered as soft away!
So unsuspected violets
Within the fields lie low,
Too late for striving fingers
That passed, an hour ago.

I never hear the word "escape"
Without a quicker blood,
A sudden expectation,
A flying attitude.

I never hear of prisons broad
By soldiers battered down,
But I tug childish at my bars,—
Only to fail again!

'Twas such a little, little boat
That toddled down the bay!
'Twas such a gallant, gallant sea
That beckoned it away!

'Twas such a greedy, greedy wave
That licked it from the coast;
Nor ever guessed the stately sails
My little craft was lost!

For each ecstatic instant
We must an anguish pay
In keen and quivering ratio
To the ecstasy.

For each beloved hour
Sharp pittances of years,
Bitter contested farthings
And coffers heaped with tears.

Surgeons must be very careful
When they take the knife!
Underneath their fine incisions
Stirs the Culprit,—Life!

A modest lot, a fame *petite*,
A brief campaign of sting and sweet
   Is plenty! Is enough!
A sailor's business is the shore,
   A soldier's-balls. Who asketh more
Must seek the neighboring life!

I taste a liquor never brewed,
From tankards scooped in pearl;
Not all the vats upon the Rhine
Yield such an alcohol!

Inebriate of air am I,
And debauchee of dew,
Reeling, through endless summer days,
From inns of molten blue.

When landlords turn the drunken bee
Out of the foxglove's door,
When butterflies renounce their drams,
I shall but drink the more!

Till seraphs swing their snowy hats,
And saints to windows run,
To see the little tippler
Leaning against the sun!

   Faith is a fine invention
   For gentlemen who see;
   But microscopes are prudent
   In an emergency!

A wounded deer leaps highest,
I've heard the hunter tell;
'Tis but the ecstasy of death,
And then the brake is still.

The smitten rock that gushes,
The trampled steel that springs:
A cheek is always redder
Just where the hectic stings!

Mirth is the mail of anguish,
In which it caution arm,
Lest anybody spy the blood
And "You're hurt" exclaim!

Portraits are to daily faces
As an evening west
To a fine, pedantic sunshine
In a satin vest.

Just lost when I was saved!
Just felt the world go by!
Just girt me for the onset with eternity,
When breath blew back,
And on the other side
I heard recede the disappointed tide!

Therefore, as one returned, I feel,
Odd secrets of the line to tell!
Some sailor, skirting foreign shores,
Some pale reporter from the awful doors
Before the seal!

Next time, to stay!
Next time, the things to see
By ear unheard,
Unscrutinized by eye.

Next time, to tarry,
While the ages steal,—
Slow tramp the centuries,
And the cycles wheel.

The thought beneath so slight a film
Is more distinctly seen,—
As laces just reveal the surge,
Or mists the Apennine.

I can wade grief,
Whole pools of it,—
I'm used to that.
But the least push of joy
Breaks up my feet,
And I tip—drunken.
Let no pebble smile,
'Twas the new liquor,—
That was all!

Power is only pain,
Stranded, through discipline,
Till weights will hang.
Give balm to giants,
And they'll wilt, like men.
Give Himmaleh,—
They'll carry him!

I'm nobody! Who are you?
Are you nobody, too?
Then there's a pair of us—don't tell!
They'd banish us, you know.
How dreary to be somebody!
How public, like a frog
To tell your name the livelong day
To an admiring bog!

Heaven is what I cannot reach!
    The apple on the tree,
Provided it do hopeless hang,
    That "heaven" is, to me.

The color on the cruising cloud,
    The interdicted ground
Behind the hill, the house behind,—
    There Paradise is found!

Hope is the thing with feathers
That perches in the soul,
And sings the tune without the words,
And never stops at all,

And sweetest in the gale is heard;
And sore must be the storm
That could abash the little bird
That kept so many warm.

I've heard it in the chillest land,
And on the strangest sea;
Yet, never, in extremity,
It asked a crumb of me.

A shady friend for torrid days
Is easier to find
Than one of higher temperature
For frigid hour of mind.

The vane a little to the east

Scares muslin souls away;
If broadcloth ... ner
Than those of o...

Who is to blame? The weaver?
Ah! the bewildering thread!
The tapestries of paradise
So noiselessly are made

We play at paste,
Till qualified for pearl,
Then drop the paste,
And deem ourself a fool.

The shapes, though, were similar,
And our new hands
Learned gem-tactics
Practicing sands.

Two poems on this page

The heart asks pleasure first,
And then, excuse from pain;
And then, those little anodynes
That deaden suffering;

And then, to go to sleep;
And then, if it should be
The will of its Inquisitor,
The liberty to die.

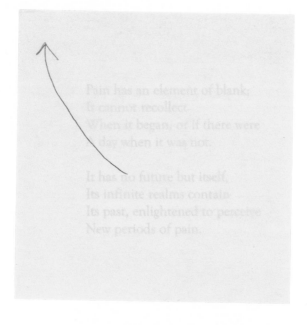

Pain has an element of blank;
It cannot recollect
When it began, or if there were
A day when it was not.

It has no future but itself,
Its infinite realms contain
Its past, enlightened to perceive
New periods of pain.

'Tis little I could care for pearls
　　Who own the ample sea;
Or brooches, when the Emperor
　　With rubies pelteth me;

Or gold, who am the Prince of Mines;
　　Or diamonds, when I see
A diadem to fit a dome
　　Continual crowning me.

I asked no other thing,
No other was denied.
I offered Being for it;
The mighty merchant smiled.

Brazil? He twirled a button.
Without a glance my way:
"But, madam, is there nothing else
That we can show today?"

I like to see it lap the miles,
And lick the valleys up,
And stop to feed itself at tanks;
And then, prodigious, step

Around a pile of mountains,
And, supercilious, peer
In shanties by the sides of roads;
And then a quarry pare

To fit its ribs, and crawl between,
Complaining all the while
In horrid, hooting stanza;
Then chase itself down hill

And neigh like Boanerges;
Then, punctual as a star,
Stop-docile and omnipotent—
At its own stable door.

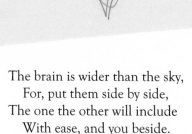

The brain is wider than the sky,
   For, put them side by side,
The one the other will include
   With ease, and you beside.

The brain is deeper than the sea,
   For, hold them, blue to blue,
The one the other will absorb,
   As sponges, buckets do.

The brain is just the weight of God,
   For, lift them, pound for pound,
And they will differ, if they do,
   As syllable from sound.

Prayer is the little implement
Through which men reach
Where presence is denied them.
They fling their speech

By means of it in God's ear;
If then He hear,
This sums the apparatus
Comprised in prayer.

To lose one's faith surpasses
    The loss of an estate,
Because estates can be
    Replenished,—faith cannot.

Inherited with life,
    Belief but once can be;
Annihilate a single clause,
    And Being's beggary.

I years had been from home,
And now, before the door,
I dared not open, lest a face
I never saw before

Stare vacant into mine
And ask my business there.
My business,—just a life I left,
Was such still dwelling there?

I fumbled at my nerve,
I scanned the windows near;
The silence like an ocean rolled,
And broke against my ear.

I laughed a wooden laugh
That I could fear a door,
Who danger and the dead had faced,
But never quaked before.

I fitted to the latch
My hand, with trembling care,
Lest back the awful door should spring,
And leave me standing there.

I moved my fingers off
As cautiously as glass,
And held my ears, and like a thief
Fled gasping from the house.

I had been hungry all the years;
My noon had come, to dine;
I, trembling, drew the table near,
And touched the curious wine.

'Twas this on tables I had seen,
When turning, hungry, lone,
I looked in windows, for the wealth
I could not hope to own.

I did not know the ample bread,
'Twas so unlike the crumb
The birds and I had often shared
In Nature's dining room.

The plenty hurt me, 'twas so new,—
Myself felt ill and odd,
As berry of a mountain bush
Transplanted to the road.

Nor was I hungry; so I found
That hunger was a way
Of persons outside windows,
The entering takes away.

Each life converges to some center
Expressed or still;
Exists in every human nature
A goal,

Embodied scarcely to itself, it may be,
Too fair
For credibility's presumption
To mar.

Adored with caution, as a brittle heaven,
To reach
Were hopeless as the rainbow's raiment
To touch,

Yet persevered toward, sure for the distance;
How high
Unto the saints' slow diligence
The sky!

Ungained, it may be, by a life's low venture,
But then,
Eternity enables the endeavoring
Again.

The body grows outside,—
The more convenient way,—
That if the spirit like to hide,
Its temple stands alway

Ajar, secure, inviting;
It never did betray
The soul that asked its shelter
In timid honesty.

The soul unto itself
Is an imperial friend,—
Or the most agonizing spy
An enemy could send.

Secure against its own,
No treason it can fear;
Itself its sovereign, of itself
The soul should stand in awe.

Is bliss, then, such abyss
I must not put my foot amiss
For fear I spoil my shoe?

I'd rather suit my foot
Than save my boot,
For yet to buy another pair
Is possible
At any fair.

But bliss is sold just once;
The patent lost
None buy it any more.

Much madness is divinest sense
To a discerning eye;
Much sense the starkest madness.
'Tis the majority
In this, as all, prevails.
Assent, and you are sane;
Demur,—you're straightway dangerous,
And handled with a chain.

Dare you see a soul at the white heat?
Then crouch within the door.
Red is the fire's common tint;
But when the vivid ore
Has vanquished flame's conditions,
It quivers from the forge,
Without a color but the light
Of unanointed blaze.
Least village has its blacksmith,
Whose anvil's even ring
Stands symbol for the finer forge
That soundless tugs within,
Refining these impatient ores
With hammer and with blaze,
Until the designated light
Repudiate the forge.

The soul selects her own society,
Then shuts the door;
To her divine majority
Present no more.

Unmoved, she notes the chariot's pausing
At her low gate;
Unmoved, an emperor be kneeling
Upon her mat.

I've known her from an ample nation
Choose one;
Then close the valves of her attention
Like stone.

I took my power in my hand
And went against the world;
'Twas not so much as David had,
But I was twice as bold.

I aimed my pebble, but myself
Was all the one that fell.
Was it Goliath was too large,
Or only I too small?

Before I got my eye put out,
I liked as well to see
As other creatures that have eyes,
And know no other way.

But were it told to me, today,
That I might have the sky
For mine, I tell you that my heart
Would split, for size of me.

The meadows mine, the mountains mine,—
All forests, stintless stars,
As much of noon as I could take
Between my finite eyes.

The motions of the dipping birds,
The lightning's jointed road,
For mine to look at when I liked,—
The news would strike me dead!

So, safer, guess, with just my soul
Upon the windowpane
Where other creatures put their eyes,
Incautious of the sun.

A precious, moldering pleasure 'tis
To meet an antique book,
In just the dress his century wore;
A privilege, I think,

His venerable hand to take,
And warming in our own,
A passage back, or two, to make
To times when he was young.

His quaint opinions to inspect,
His knowledge to unfold
On what concerns our mutual mind,
The literature of old;

What interested scholars most,
What competitions ran
When Plato was a certainty,
And Sophocles a man;

When Sappho was a living girl,
And Beatrice wore
The gown that Dante deified.
Facts, centuries before,

He traverses familiar,
As one should come to town
And tell you all your dreams were true:
He lived where dreams were born.

His presence is enchantment,
You beg him not to go;
Old volumes shake their vellum heads
And tantalize, just so.

Unto my books so good to turn
Far ends of tired days;
It half endears the abstinence,
And pain is missed in praise.

As flavors cheer retarded guests
With banquetings to be,
So spices stimulate the time
Till my small library.

It may be wilderness without,
Far feet of failing men,
But holiday excludes the night,
And it is bells within.

I thank these kinsmen of the shelf;
Their countenances bland
Enamor in prospective,
And satisfy, obtained.

I many times thought peace had come,
When peace was far away;
As wrecked men deem they sight the land
At center of the sea,

And struggle slacker, but to prove,
As hopelessly as I,
How many the fictitious shores
Before the harbor lie.

Remorse is memory awake,
Her companies astir,—
A presence of departed acts
At window and at door.

Its past set down before the soul,
And lighted with a match,
Perusal to facilitate
Of its condensed despatch.

Remorse is cureless,—the disease
Not even God can heal;
For 'tis his institution,—
The complement of hell.

God gave a loaf to every bird,
But just a crumb to me;
I dare not eat it, though I starve,—
My poignant luxury
To own it, touch it, prove the feat
That made the pellet mine,—
Too happy in my sparrow chance
For ampler coveting.

It might be famine all around,
I could not miss an ear,
Such plenty smiles upon my board,
My garner shows so fair.
I wonder how the rich may feel,—
An Indiaman—an Earl?
I deem that I with but a crumb
Am sovereign of them all.

Through the strait pass of suffering
The martyrs even trod,
Their feet upon temptation,
Their faces upon God.

A stately, shriven company;
Convulsion playing round,
Harmless as streaks of meteor
Upon a planet's bond.

Their faith the everlasting troth;
Their expectation fair;
The needle to the north degree
Wades so, through polar air.

I felt a cleavage in my mind
   As if my brain had split;
I tried to match it, seam by seam,
   But could not make them fit.

The thought behind I strove to join
   Unto the thought before,
But sequence raveled out of reach
   Like balls upon a floor.

I stepped from plank to plank
   So slow and cautiously;
The stars about my head I felt,
   About my feet the sea.

I knew not but the next
   Would be my final inch,—
This gave me that precarious gait
   Some call experience.

If I can stop one heart from breaking,
I shall not live in vain;
If I can ease one life the aching,
Or cool one pain,
Or help one fainting robin
Unto his nest again,
I shall not live in vain.

Fate slew him, but he did not drop;
   She felled—he did not fall—
Impaled him on her fiercest stakes—
   He neutralized them all.

She stung him, sapped his firm advance,
   But, when her worst was done,
And he, unmoved, regarded her,
   Acknowledged him a man.

Superiority to fate
    Is difficult to learn.
'Tis not conferred by any,
    But possible to earn

A pittance at a time,
    Until, to her surprise,
The soul with strict economy
    Subsists till Paradise.

A word is dead
When it is said,
    Some say.
I say it just
Begins to live
    That day.

A thought went up my mind today
That I have had before,
But did not finish,—some way back,
I could not fix the year,

Nor where it went, nor why it came
The second time to me,
Nor definitely what it was,
Have I the art to say.

But somewhere in my soul, I know
I've met the thing before;
It just reminded me—'twas all—
And came my way no more.

There is no frigate like a book
To take us lands away,
Nor any coursers like a page
Of prancing poetry.

This traverse may the poorest take
Without oppress of toll;
How frugal is the chariot
That bears a human soul!

Is Heaven a physician?
They say that He can heal;
But medicine posthumous
Is unavailable.

Is Heaven an exchequer?
They speak of what we owe;
But that negotiation
I'm not a party to.

I worked for chaff, and earning wheat
Was haughty and betrayed.
What right had fields to arbitrate
In matters ratified?

I tasted wheat,—and hated chaff,
And thanked the ample friend;
Wisdom is more becoming viewed
At distance than at hand.

Forbidden fruit a flavor has
   That lawful orchards mocks;
How luscious lies the pea within
   The pod that Duty locks!

Who never wanted,—maddest joy
   Remains to him unknown;
The banquet of abstemiousness
   Surpasses that of wine.

Within its hope, though yet ungrasped
   Desire's perfect goal,
No nearer, lest reality
   Should disenthrall thy soul.

The reticent volcano keeps
   His never slumbering plan;
Confided are his projects pink
   To no precarious man.

If nature will not tell the tale
   Jehovah told to her,
Can human nature not survive
   Without a listener?

Admonished by her buckled lips
   Let every babbler be.
The only secret people keep
   Is Immortality.

Hope is a subtle glutton;
   He feeds upon the fair;
And yet, inspected closely,
   What abstinence is there!

His is the halcyon table
   That never seats but one,
And whatsoever is consumed
   The same amounts remain.

The farthest thunder that I heard
   Was nearer than the sky,
And rumbles still, though torrid noons
   Have lain their missiles by.
The lightning that preceded it
   Struck no one but myself,
But I would not exchange the bolt
   For all the rest of life.
Indebtedness to oxygen
   The chemist may repay,
But not the obligation
   To electricity.
It founds the homes and decks the days,
   And every clamor bright
Is but the gleam concomitant
   Of that waylaying light.
The thought is quiet as a flake,—
   A crash without a sound;
How life's reverberation
   Its explanation found!

He ate and drank the precious words,
His spirit grew robust;
He knew no more that he was poor,
Nor that his frame was dust.
He danced along the dingy days,
And this bequest of wings
Was but a book. What liberty
A loosened spirit brings!

My life closed twice before its close;
    It yet remains to see
If Immortality unveil
    A third event to me,

So huge, so hopeless to conceive,
    As these that twice befell.
Parting is all we know of heaven,
    And all we need of hell.

LOVE

It's all I have to bring today,
  This, and my heart beside,
This, and my heart, and all the fields,
  And all the meadows wide.
Be sure you count, should I forget,—
  Some one the sum could tell,—
This, and my heart, and all the bees
  Which in the clover dwell.

There is a word
Which bears a sword
  Can pierce an armed man.
It hurls its barbed syllables,—
  At once is mute again.
But where it fell
The saved will tell
  On patriotic day,
Some epauletted brother
  Gave his breath away.

Wherever runs the breathless sun,
  Wherever roams the day,
There is its noiseless onset,
  There is its victory!
Behold the keenest marksman!
  The most accomplished shot!
Time's sublimest target
  Is a soul "forgot"!

Heart, we will forget him!
  You and I, tonight!
You may forget the warmth he gave,
  I will forget the light.

When you have done, pray tell me,
  That I my thoughts may dim;
Haste! lest while you're lagging,
  I may remember him!

When roses cease to bloom, dear,
　And violets are done,
When bumblebees in solemn flight
　Have passed beyond the sun,

The hand that paused to gather
　Upon this summer's day
Will idle lie, in Auburn,—
　Then take my flower, pray!

Did the harebell loose her girdle
To the lover bee,
Would the bee the harebell hallow
Much as formerly?

Did the paradise, persuaded,
Yield her moat of pearl,
Would the Eden be an Eden,
Or the earl an earl?

Come slowly, Eden!
Lips unused to thee,
Bashful, sip thy jasmines,
As the fainting bee,

Reaching late his flower,
Round her chamber hums,
Counts his nectars—enters,
And is lost in balms!

I'm wife; I've finished that,
That other state;
I'm Czar, I'm woman now:
It's safer so.

How odd the girl's life looks
Behind this soft eclipse!
I think that earth feels so
To folks in heaven now.

This being comfort, then
That other kind was pain;
But why compare?
I'm wife! stop there!

Father, I bring thee not myself,—
   That were the little load;
I bring thee the imperial heart
   I had not strength to hold.

The heart I cherished in my own
   Till mine too heavy grew,
Yet strangest, heavier since it went,
   Is it too large for you?

What if I say I shall not wait?
What if I burst the fleshly gate
And pass, escaped, to thee?

What if I file this mortal off,
See where it hurt me,—that's enough,—
And wade in liberty?

They cannot take us any more,—
Dungeons can call, and guns implore;
Unmeaning now, to me,

As laughter was an hour ago,
Or laces, or a travelling show,
Or who died yesterday!

I held a jewel in my fingers
And went to sleep.
The day was warm, and winds were prosy;
I said: " 'Twill keep."

I woke and chid my honest fingers,—
The gem was gone;
And now an amethyst remembrance
Is all I own.

Doubt me, my dim companion!
Why, God would be content
With but a fraction of the love
Poured thee without a stint.
The whole of me, forever,
What more the woman can,—
Say quick, that I may dower thee
With last delight I own!

It cannot be my spirit,
For that was thine before;
I ceded all of dust I knew,—
What opulence the more
Had I, a humble maiden,
Whose farthest of degree
Was that she might,
Some distant heaven,
Dwell timidly with thee!

Wild nights! Wild nights!
Were I with thee,
Wild nights should be
Our luxury!

Futile the winds
To a heart in port,—
Done with the compass,
Done with the chart.

Rowing in Eden!
Ah! the sea!
Might I but moor tonight
In thee!

A charm invests a face
Imperfectly beheld,—
The lady dare not lift her veil
For fear it be dispelled.

But peers beyond her mesh,
And wishes, and denies,—
Lest interview annul a want
That image satisfies.

I live with him, I see his face;
　　I go no more away
For visitor, or sundown;
　　Death's single privacy,

The only one forestalling mine,
　　And that by right that he
Presents a claim invisible,
　　No wedlock granted me.

I live with him, I hear his voice,
　　I stand alive today
To witness to the certainty
　　Of immortality

Taught me by Time,—the lower way,
　　Conviction every day,—
That life like this is endless,
　　Be judgment what it may.

A solemn thing it was, I said,
  A woman white to be,
And wear, if God should count me fit,
  Her hallowed mystery.
A timid thing to drop a life
  Into the purple well,
Too plummetless that it come back
  Eternity until.

The moon is distant from the sea,
And yet with amber hands
She leads him, docile as a boy,
Along appointed sands.

He never misses a degree;
Obedient to her eye,
He comes just so far toward the town,
Just so far goes away.

Oh, Signor, thine the amber hand,
And mine the distant sea,—
Obedient to the least command
Thine eyes impose on me.

Mine by the right of the white election!
Mine by the royal seal!
Mine by the sign in the scarlet prison
Bars cannot conceal!

Mine, here in vision and in veto!
Mine, by the grave's repeal
Titled, confirmed,—delirious charter!
Mine, while the ages steal!

I'm ceded, I've stopped being theirs;
The name they dropped upon my face
With water, in the country church,
Is finished using now,
And they can put it with my dolls,
My childhood, and the string of spools
I've finished threading too.

Baptized before without the choice,
But this time consciously, of grace
Unto supremest name,
Called to my full, the crescent dropped,
Existence's whole arc filled up
With one small diadem.

My second rank, too small the first,
Crowned, crowing on my father's breast,
A half unconscious queen;
But this time, adequate, erect,
With will to choose or to reject,
And I choose—just a throne.

I envy seas whereon he rides,
  I envy spokes of wheels
Of chariots that him convey,
  I envy speechless hills

That gaze upon his journey;
  How easy all can see
What is forbidden utterly
  As heaven, unto me!

I envy nests of sparrows
  That dot his distant eaves,
The wealthy fly upon his pane,
  The happy, happy leaves

That just abroad his window
  Have summer's leave to be,
The earrings of Pizarro
  Could not obtain for me.

I envy light that wakes him,
  And bells that boldly ring
To tell him it is noon abroad,—
  Myself his noon could bring,

Yet interdict my blossom
  And abrogate my bee,
Lest noon in everlasting night
  Drop Gabriel and me.

If you were coming in the fall,
I'd brush the summer by
With half a smile and half a spurn,
As housewives do a fly.

If I could see you in a year,
I'd wind the months in balls,
And put them each in separate drawers,
Until their time befalls.

If only centuries delayed,
I'd count them on my hand,
Subtracting till my fingers dropped
Into Van Diemen's Land.

If certain, when this life was out,
That yours and mine should be,
I'd toss it yonder like a rind,
And taste eternity.

But now, all ignorant of the length
Of time's uncertain wing,
It goads me, like the goblin bee,
That will not state its sting.

That I did always love,
I bring thee proof:
That till I loved
I did not love enough.

That I shall love alway,
I offer thee
That love is life,
And life hath immortality.

This, dost thou doubt, sweet?
Then have I
Nothing to show
But Calvary.

I gave myself to him,
And took himself for pay.
The solemn contract of a life
Was ratified this way.
The wealth might disappoint,
Myself a poorer prove
Than this great purchaser suspect:
The daily own of Love
Depreciate the vision;
But, till the merchant buy,
Still fable, in the isles of spice,
The subtle cargoes lie.
At least, 'tis mutual risk,—
Some found it mutual gain;
Sweet debt of Life,—each night to owe,
Insolvent, every noon.

'Twas a long parting, but the time
For interview had come;
Before the judgment seat of God,
The last and second time

These fleshless lovers met,
A heaven in a gaze,
A heaven of heavens, the privilege
Of one another's eyes.

No lifetime set on them,
Apparelled as the new
Unborn, except they had beheld,
Born everlasting now.

Was bridal e'er like this?
A paradise, the host,
And cherubim and seraphim
The most familiar guest.

I cannot live with you,
It would be life,
And life is over there
Behind the shelf

The sexton keeps the key to,
Putting up
Our life, his porcelain,
Like a cup

Discarded of the housewife,
Quaint or broken;
A newer Sevres pleases,
Old ones crack.

I could not die with you,
For one must wait
To shut the other's gaze down,—
You could not.

And I, could I stand by
And see you freeze,
Without my right of frost,
Death's privilege?

Nor could I rise with you,
Because your face
Would put out Jesus',
That new grace

Glow plain and foreign
On my homesick eye,
Except that you, than he
Shone closer by.

They'd judge us—how?
For you served Heaven, you know,
Or sought to;
I could not,

Because you saturated sight,
And I had no more eyes
For sordid excellence
As Paradise.

And were you lost, I would be,
Though my name
Rang loudest
On the heavenly fame.

And were you saved,
And I condemned to be
Where you were not,
That self were hell to me.

So we must keep apart,
You there, I here,
With just the door ajar
That oceans are,
And prayer,
And that pale sustenance,
Despair.

Of all the souls that stand create
I have elected one.
When sense from spirit files away,
And subterfuge is done;

When that which is and that which was
Apart, intrinsic, stand,
And this brief tragedy of flesh
Is shifted like a sand;

When figures show their royal front
And mists are carved away,—
Behold the atom I preferred
To all the lists of clay!

He fumbles at your spirit
    As players at the keys
Before they drop full music on;
    He stuns you by degrees,

Prepares your brittle substance
    For the ethereal blow,
By fainter hammers, further heard,
    Then nearer, then so slow

Your breath has time to straighten,
    Your brain to bubble cool,—
Deals one imperial thunderbolt
    That scalps your naked soul.

The way I read a letter's this:
'Tis first I lock the door,
And push it with my fingers next,
For transport it be sure.

And then I go the furthest off
To counteract a knock;
Then draw my little letter forth
And softly pick its lock.

Then, glancing narrow at the wall,
And narrow at the floor,
For firm conviction of a mouse
Not exorcised before,

Peruse how infinite I am
To no one that you know!
And sigh for lack of heaven,—but not
The heaven the creeds bestow.

He touched me, so I live to know
That such a day, permitted so,
    I groped upon his breast.
It was a boundless place to me,
And silenced, as the awful sea
    Puts minor streams to rest.

And now, I'm different from before,
As if I breathed superior air,
    Or brushed a royal gown;
My feet, too, that had wandered so,
My gypsy face transfigured now
    To tenderer renown.

Alter? When the hills do.
Falter? When the sun
Question if his glory
Be the perfect one.

Surfeit? When the daffodil
Doth of the dew:
Even as herself, O friend!
I will of you!

One blessing had I, than the rest
    So larger to my eyes
That I stopped gauging, satisfied,
    For this enchanted size.

It was the limit of my dream,
    The focus of my prayer,—
A perfect, paralyzing bliss
    Contented as despair.

I knew no more of want or cold,
    Phantasms both become,
For this new value in the soul,
    Supremest earthly sum.

The heaven below the heaven above
    Obscured with ruddier hue.
Life's latitude leant over-full;
    The judgment perished, too.

Why joys so scantily disburse,
    Why Paradise defer,
Why floods are served to us in bowls,—
    I speculate no more.

She rose to his requirement, dropped
The playthings of her life
To take the honorable work
Of woman and of wife.

If aught she missed in her new day
Of amplitude, or awe,
Or first prospective, or the gold
In using wore away,

It lay unmentioned, as the sea
Develops pearl and weed,
But only to himself is known
The fathoms they abide.

We outgrow love like other things
And put it in the drawer,
Till it an antique fashion shows
Like costumes grandsires wore.

Split the lark and you'll find the music,
Bulb after bulb, in silver rolled,
Scantily dealt to the summer morning,
Saved for your ear when lutes be old.

Loose the flood, you shall find it patent,
Gush after gush, reserved for you;
Scarlet experiment! sceptic Thomas,
Now, do you doubt that your bird was true?

I hide myself within my flower,
That wearing on your breast,
You, unsuspecting, wear me too—
And angels know the rest.

I hide myself within my flower,
That, fading from your vase,
You, unsuspecting, feel for me
Almost a loneliness.

Not with a club the heart is broken,
    Nor with a stone;
A whip, so small you could not see it,
    I've known

To lash the magic creature
    Till it fell,
Yet that whip's name too noble
    Then to tell.

Magnanimous of bird
    By boy descried,
To sing unto the stone
    Of which it died.

Love is anterior to life,
Posterior to death,
Initial of creation, and
The exponent of breath.

I have no life but this,
To lead it here;
Nor any death, but lest
Dispelled from there;

Nor tie to earths to come,
Nor action new,
Except through this extent,
The realm of you.

I've got an arrow here;
Loving the hand that sent it,
I the dart revere.

Fell, they will say, in "skirmish"!
Vanquished, my soul will know,
By but a simple arrow
Sped by an archer's bow.

Proud of my broken heart since thou didst break it,
   Proud of the pain I did not feel till thee,
Proud of my night since thou with moons dost slake it,
   Not to partake thy passion, my humility.

Elysium is as far as to
The very nearest room,
If in that room a friend await
Felicity or doom.

What fortitude the soul contains,
That it can so endure
The accent of a coming foot,
The opening of a door!

NATURE

My nosegays are for captives;
Dim, long-expectant eyes,
Fingers denied the plucking,
Patient till paradise.

To such, if they should whisper
Of morning and the moor,
They bear no other errand,
And I, no other prayer.

The gentian weaves her fringes,
The maple's loom is red.
My departing blossoms
Obviate parade.

A brief, but patient illness,
An hour to prepare;
And one, below this morning,
Is where the angels are.

It was a short procession,—
The bobolink was there,
An aged bee addressed us,
And then we knelt in prayer.

We trust that she was willing,—
We ask that we may be.
Summer, sister, seraph,
Let us go with thee!

In the name of the bee
And of the butterfly
And of the breeze, amen

Bring me the sunset in a cup,
Reckon the morning's flagons up,
    And say how many dew;
Tell me how far the morning leaps,
Tell me what time the weaver sleeps
    Who spun the breadths of blue!

Write me how many notes there be
In the new robin's ecstasy
    Among astonished boughs;
How many trips the tortoise makes,
How many cups the bee partakes,—
    The debauchee of dews!

Also, who laid the rainbow's piers,
Also, who leads the docile spheres
    By withes of supple blue?
Whose fingers string the stalactite,
Who counts the wampum of the night,
    To see that none is due?

Who built this little Alban house
And shut the windows down so close
    My spirit cannot see?
Who'll let me out some gala day,
With implements to fly away,
    Passing pomposity?

These are the days when birds come back,
A very few, a bird or two,
To take a backward look.

These are the days when skies put on
The old, old sophistries of June,—
A blue and gold mistake.

Oh, fraud that cannot cheat the bee,
Almost thy plausibility
Induces my belief,

Till ranks of seeds their witness bear,
And softly through the altered air
Hurries a timid leaf!

Oh, sacrament of summer days,
Oh, last communion in the haze,
Permit a child to join,

Thy sacred emblems to partake,
Thy consecrated bread to break,
Taste thine immortal wine!

An altered look about the hills;
A Tyrian light the village fills;
A wider sunrise in the dawn;
A deeper twilight on the lawn;
A print of a vermilion foot;
A purple finger on the slope;
A flippant fly upon the pane;
A spider at his trade again;
An added strut in chanticleer;
A flower expected everywhere;
An axe shrill singing in the woods;
Fern-odors on untraveled roads,—
All this, and more I cannot tell,
A furtive look you know as well,
And Nicodemus' mystery
Receives its annual reply.

Perhaps you'd like to buy a flower?
But I could never sell.
If you would like to borrow
Until the daffodil

Unties her yellow bonnet
Beneath the village door,
Until the bees, from clover rows
Their hock and sherry draw,

Why, I will lend until just then,
But not an hour more!

Besides the autumn poets sing,
A few prosaic days
A little this side of the snow
And that side of the haze.

A few incisive mornings,
A few ascetic eves,—
Gone Mr. Bryant's goldenrod,
And Mr. Thomson's sheaves.

Still is the bustle in the brook,
Sealed are the spicy valves;
Mesmeric fingers softly touch
The eyes of many elves.

Perhaps a squirrel may remain,
My sentiments to share.
Grant me, O Lord, a sunny mind,
Thy windy will to bear!

I'll tell you how the sun rose,—
A ribbon at a time.
The steeples swam in amethyst,
The news like squirrels ran.

The hills untied their bonnets,
The bobolinks begun.
Then I said softly to myself,
"That must have been the sun!"

But how he set, I know not.
There seemed a purple stile
That little yellow boys and girls
Were climbing all the while

Till when they reached the other side,
A dominie in gray
Put gently up the evening bars,
And led the flock away.

Some keep the Sabbath going to church;
I keep it staying at home,
With a bobolink for a chorister,
And an orchard for a dome.

Some keep the Sabbath in surplice;
I just wear my wings,
And instead of tolling the bell for church,
Our little sexton sings.

God preaches,—a noted clergyman,—
And the sermon is never long;
So instead of getting to heaven at last,
I'm going all along!

This is the land the sunset washes,
These are the banks of the Yellow Sea;
Where it rose, or whither it rushes,
These are the western mystery!

Night after night her purple traffic
Strews the landing with opal bales;
Merchantmen poise upon horizons,
Dip, and vanish with fairy sails.

She sweeps with many-colored brooms,
And leaves the shreds behind;
Oh, housewife in the evening west,
Come back, and dust the pond!

You dropped a purple ravelling in,
You dropped an amber thread;
And now you've littered all the East
With duds of emerald!

And still she plies her spotted brooms,
And still the aprons fly,
Till brooms fade softly into stars—
And then I come away.

Where ships of purple gently toss
On seas of daffodil,
Fantastic sailors mingle,
And then—the wharf is still.

It can't be summer,—that got through;
It's early yet for spring;
There's that long town of white to cross
Before the blackbirds sing.
It can't be dying,—it's too rouge,—
The dead shall go in white.
So sunset shuts my question down
With clasps of chrysolite.

Blazing in gold and quenching in purple,
Leaping like leopards to the sky,
Then at the feet of the old horizon
Laying her spotted face, to die;

Stooping as low as the otter's window,
Touching the roof and tinting the barn,
Kissing her bonnet to the meadow,—
And the juggler of day is gone!

Of bronze and blaze
The north, tonight!
   So adequate it forms,
So preconcerted with itself,
   So distant to alarms,—
An unconcern so sovereign
   To universe, or me,
It paints my simple spirit
   With tints of majesty,
Till I take vaster attitudes,
   And strut upon my stem,
Disdaining men and oxygen,
   For arrogance of them.

My splendors are menagerie;
   But their competeless show
Will entertain the centuries
   When I am, long ago,
An island in dishonored grass,
   Whom none but beetles know.

There's a certain slant of light,
On winter afternoons,
That oppresses, like the heft
Of cathedral tunes.

Heavenly hurt it gives us;
We can find no scar,
But internal difference
Where the meanings are.

None may teach it anything,
'Tis the seal, despair,—
An imperial affliction
Sent us of the air.

When it comes, the landscape listens,
Shadows hold their breath;
When it goes, 'tis like the distance
On the look of death.

How the old mountains drip with sunset,
   How the hemlocks burn,
How the dun brake is draped in cinder
   By the wizard sun!

How the old steeples hand the scarlet,
   Till the ball is full,—
Have I the lip of the flamingo
   That I dare to tell?

Then, how the fire ebbs like billows,
   Touching all the grass
With a departing, sapphire feature,
   As if a duchess passed!

How a small dusk crawls on the village
   Till the houses blot;
And the odd flambeau no men carry
   Glimmer on the street!

How it is night in nest and kennel,
   And where was the wood,
Just a dome of abyss is bowing
   Into solitude!—

These are the visions flitted Guido;
   Titian never told;
Domenichino dropped his pencil,
   Paralyzed with gold.

The day came slow, till five o'clock,
Then sprang before the hills
Like hindered rubies, or the light
A sudden musket spills.

The purple could not keep the east,
The sunrise shook from fold,
Like breadths of topaz, packed a night,
The lady just unrolled.

The happy winds their timbrels took;
The birds, in docile rows,
Arranged themselves around their prince—
(The wind is prince of those).

The orchard sparkled like a Jew,—
How mighty 'twas, to stay
A guest in this stupendous place,
The parlor of the day!

Pink, small, and punctual.
Aromatic, low,
Covert in April,
Candid in May,

Dear to the moss,
Known by the knoll,
Next to the robin
In every human soul.

Bold little beauty,
Bedecked with thee,
Nature forswears
Antiquity.

Of all the sounds despatched abroad,
There's not a charge to me
Like that old measure in the boughs,
That phraseless melody

The wind does, working like a hand
Whose fingers brush the sky,
Then quiver down, with tufts of tune
Permitted gods and me.

When winds go round and round in bands,
And thrum upon the door,
And birds take places overhead,
To bear them orchestra,

I crave him grace, of summer boughs,
If such an outcast be,
He never heard that fleshless chant
Rise solemn in the tree,

As if some caravan of sound
On deserts, in the sky,
Had broken rank,
Then knit, and passed
In seamless company.

A bird came down the walk:
He did not know I saw;
He bit an angleworm in halves
And ate the fellow, raw.

And then he drank a dew
From a convenient grass,
And then hopped sidewise to the wall
To let a beetle pass.

He glanced with rapid eyes
That hurried all abroad,—
They looked like frightened beads, I thought;
He stirred his velvet head

Like one in danger; cautious,
I offered him a crumb,
And he unrolled his feathers
And rowed him softer home

Than oars divide the ocean,
Too silver for a seam,
Or butterflies, off banks of noon,
Leap, plashless, as they swim.

I dreaded that first robin so,
But he is mastered now,
And I'm accustomed to him grown,—
He hurts a little, though.

I thought if I could only live
Till that first shout got by,
Not all pianos in the woods
Had power to mangle me.

I dared not meet the daffodils,
For fear their yellow gown
Would pierce me with a fashion
So foreign to my own.

I wished the grass would hurry,
So when 'twas time to see,
He'd be too tall, the tallest one
Could stretch to look at me.

I could not bear the bees should come,
I wished they'd stay away
In those dim countries where they go:
What word had they for me?

They're here, though; not a creature failed,
No blossom stayed away
In gentle deference to me,
The Queen of Calvary.

Each one salutes me as he goes,
And I my childish plumes
Lift, in bereaved acknowledgment
Of their unthinking drums.

The grass so little has to do,—
A sphere of simple green,
With only butterflies to brood,
And bees to entertain,

And stir all day to pretty tunes
The breezes fetch along,
And hold the sunshine in its lap
And bow to everything;

And thread the dews all night, like pearls,
And make itself so fine,—
A duchess were too common
For such a noticing.

And even when it dies, to pass
In odors so divine,
As lowly spices gone to sleep,
Or amulets of pine.

And then to dwell in sovereign barns,
And dream the days away,—
The grass so little has to do,
I wish I were the hay!

A murmur in the trees to note,
   Not loud enough for wind;
A star not far enough to seek,
   Nor near enough to find;

A long, long yellow on the lawn,
   A hubbub as of feet;
Not audible, as ours to us,
   But dapperer, more sweet;

A hurrying home of little men
   To houses unperceived,—
All this, and more, if I should tell,
   Would never be believed.

Of robins in the trundle bed
   How many I espy
Whose nightgowns could not hide the wings,
   Although I heard them try!

But then I promised ne'er to tell;
   How could I break my word?
So go your way and I'll go mine,—
   No fear you'll miss the road.

The wind tapped like a tired man,
And like a host, "Come in,"
I boldly answered; entered then
My residence within

A rapid, footless guest,
To offer whom a chair
Were as impossible as hand
A sofa to the air.

No bone had he to bind him,
His speech was like the push
Of numerous hummingbirds at once
From a superior bush.

His countenance a billow,
His fingers, if he pass,
Let go a music, as of tunes
Blown tremulous in glass.

He visited, still flitting;
Then, like a timid man,
Again he tapped—'twas flurriedly—
And I became alone.

I started early, took my dog,
And visited the sea;
The mermaids in the basement
Came out to look at me,

And frigates in the upper floor
Extended hempen hands,
Presuming me to be a mouse
Aground, upon the sands.

But no man moved me till the tide
Went past my simple shoe,
And past my apron and my belt,
And past my bodice too,

And made as he would eat me up
As wholly as a dew
Upon a dandelion's sleeve—
And then I started too.

And he—he followed close behind;
I felt his silver heel
Upon my ankle,—then my shoes
Would overflow with pearl.

Until we met the solid town,
No man he seemed to know;
And bowing with a mighty look
At me, the sea withdrew.

God made a little gentian;
It tried to be a rose
And failed, and all the summer laughed.
But just before the snows
There came a purple creature
That ravished all the hill;
And summer hid her forehead,
And mockery was still.
The frosts were her condition;
The Tyrian would not come
Until the North evoked it.
"Creator! shall I bloom?"

Like mighty footlights burned the red
At bases of the trees,—
The far theatricals of day
Exhibiting to these.

'Twas universe that did applaud
While, chiefest of the crowd,
Enabled by his royal dress,
Myself distinguished God.

Two butterflies went out at noon
And waltzed above a stream,
Then stepped straight through the firmament
And rested on a beam;

And then together bore away
Upon a shining sea,—
Though never yet, in any port,
Their coming mentioned be.

If spoken by the distant bird,
If met in ether sea
By frigate or by merchantman,
Report was not to me.

It makes no difference abroad,
The seasons fit the same,
The mornings blossom into noons,
And split their pods of flame.

Wildflowers kindle in the woods,
The brooks brag all the day;
No blackbird bates his jargoning
For passing Calvary.

Auto-da-fe and judgment
Are nothing to the bee;
His separation from his rose
To him seems misery.

Could I but ride indefinite,
  As doth the meadow bee,
And visit only where I liked,
  And no man visit me,

And flirt all day with buttercups,
  And marry whom I may,
And dwell a little everywhere,
  Or better, run away

With no police to follow,
  Or chase me if I do,
Till I should jump peninsulas
  To get away from you,—

I said, but just to be a bee
  Upon a raft of air,
And row in nowhere all day long,
  And anchor off the bar,—

What liberty! So captives deem
  Who tight in dungeons are.

The moon was but a chin of gold
    A night or two ago,
And now she turns her perfect face
    Upon the world below.

Her forehead is of amplest blond;
    Her cheek like beryl stone;
Her eye unto the summer dew
    The likest I have known.

Her lips of amber never part;
    But what must be the smile
Upon her friend she could bestow
    Were such her silver will!

And what a privilege to be
    But the remotest star!
For certainly her way might pass
    Beside your twinkling door.

Her bonnet is the firmament,
    The universe her shoe,
The stars the trinkets at her belt,
    Her dimities of blue.

Nature, the gentlest mother,
Impatient of no child,
The feeblest or the waywardest,—
Her admonition mild

In forest and the hill
By traveler is heard,
Restraining rampant squirrel
Or too impetuous bird.

How fair her conversation,
A summer afternoon,—
Her household, her assembly;
And when the sun goes down

Her voice among the aisles
Incites the timid prayer
Of the minutest cricket,
The most unworthy flower.

When all the children sleep
She turns as long away
As will suffice to light her lamps;
Then, bending from the sky,

With infinite affection
And infiniter care,
Her golden finger on her lip,
Wills silence everywhere.

A drop fell on the apple tree,
Another on the roof;
A half a dozen kissed the eaves,
And made the gables laugh.

A few went out to help the brook,
That went to help the sea.
Myself conjectured, Were they pearls,
What necklaces could be!

The dust replaced in hoisted roads,
The birds jocoser sung;
The sunshine threw his hat away,
The orchards spangles hung.

The breezes brought dejected lutes,
And bathed them in the glee;
The East put out a single flag,
And signed the fete away.

A light exists in spring
    Not present on the year
At any other period.
    When March is scarcely here

A color stands abroad
    On solitary hills
That science cannot overtake,
    But human nature *feels.*

It waits upon the lawn;
    It shows the furthest tree
Upon the furthest slope we know;
    It almost speaks to me.

Then, as horizons step,
    Or noons report away,
Without the formula of sound,
    It passes, and we stay:

A quality of loss
    Affecting our content,
As trade had suddenly encroached
    Upon a sacrament.

The wind begun to rock the grass
With threatening tunes and low,—
He flung a menace at the earth,
A menace at the sky.

The leaves unhooked themselves from trees
And started all abroad;
The dust did scoop itself like hands
And throw away the road.

The wagons quickened on the streets,
The thunder hurried slow;
The lightning showed a yellow beak,
And then a livid claw.

The birds put up the bars to nests,
The cattle fled to barns;
There came one drop of giant rain,
And then, as if the hands

That held the dams had parted hold,
The waters wrecked the sky,
But overlooked my father's house,
Just quartering a tree.

The mountain sat upon the plain
In his eternal chair,
His observation omnifold,
His inquest everywhere.

The seasons prayed around his knees,
Like children round a sire:
Grandfather of the days is he,
Of dawn the ancestor.

An everywhere of silver,
With ropes of sand
To keep it from effacing
The track called land.

Drab habitation of whom?
Tabernacle or tomb,
Or dome of worm,
Or porch of gnome,
Or some elf's catacomb?

A narrow fellow in the grass
Occasionally rides;
You may have met him,—did you not,
His notice sudden is.

The grass divides as with a comb,
A spotted shaft is seen;
And then it closes at your feet
And opens further on.

He likes a boggy acre,
A floor too cool for corn.
Yet when a child, and barefoot,
I more than once, at morn,

Have passed, I thought, a whiplash
Unbraiding in the sun,—
When, stooping to secure it,
It wrinkled, and was gone.

Several of nature's people
I know, and they know me;
I feel for them a transport
Of cordiality;

But never met this fellow,
Attended or alone,
Without a tighter breathing,
And zero at the bone.

Nature rarer uses yellow
    Than another hue;
Saves she all of that for sunsets,—
    Prodigal of blue,

Spending scarlet like a woman,
    Yellow she affords
Only scantly and selectly,
    Like a lover's words.

The crickets sang,
And set the sun,
And workmen finished, one by one,
    Their seam the day upon.

The low grass loaded with the dew,
The twilight stood as strangers do
With hat in hand, polite and new,
    To stay as if, or go.

A vastness, as a neighbor, came,—
A wisdom without face or name,
A peace, as hemispheres at home,—
    And so the night became.

Farther in summer than the birds,
Pathetic from the grass,
A minor nation celebrates
Its unobtrusive mass.

No ordinance is seen,
So gradual the grace,
A pensive custom it becomes,
Enlarging loneliness.

Antiquest felt at noon
When August, burning low,
Calls forth this spectral canticle,
Repose to typify.

Remit as yet no grace,
No furrow on the glow,
Yet a druidic difference
Enhances nature now.

A spider sewed at night
Without a light
Upon an arc of white.
If ruff it was of dame
Or shroud of gnome,
Himself, himself inform.
Of immortality
His strategy
Was physiognomy.

The spider as an artist
   Has never been employed
Though his surpassing merit
   Is freely certified

By every broom and Bridget
   Throughout a Christian land.
Neglected son of genius,
   I take thee by the hand.

Like trains of cars on tracks of plush
I hear the level bee:
A jar across the flowers goes,
Their velvet masonry

Withstands until the sweet assault
Their chivalry consumes,
While he, victorious, tilts away
To vanquish other blooms.

His feet are shod with gauze,
His helmet is of gold;
His breast, a single onyx
With chrysoprase, inlaid.

His labor is a chant,
His idleness a tune;
Oh, for a bee's experience
Of clovers and of noon!

Dear March, come in!
How glad I am!
I looked for you before.
Put down your hat—
You must have walked—
How out of breath you are!
Dear March, how are you?
And the rest?
Did you leave Nature well?
Oh, March, come right upstairs with me,
I have so much to tell!

I got your letter, and the birds';
The maples never knew
That you were coming,—I declare,
How red their faces grew!
But, March, forgive me—
And all those hills
You left for me to hue;
There was no purple suitable,
You took it all with you.

Who knocks? That April!
Lock the door!
I will not be pursued!
He stayed away a year, to call
When I am occupied.
But trifles look so trivial
As soon as you have come,
That blame is just as dear as praise
And praise as mere as blame.

The mushroom is the elf of plants,
At evening it is not;
At morning in a truffled hut
It stop upon a spot

As if it tarried always;
And yet its whole career
Is shorter than a snake's delay,
And fleeter than a tare.

'Tis vegetation's juggler,
The germ of alibi;
Doth like a bubble antedate,
And like a bubble hie.

I feel as if the grass were pleased
To have it intermit;
The surreptitious scion
Of summer's circumspect.

Had nature any outcast face,
Could she a son contemn,
Had nature an Iscariot,
That mushroom,—it is him!

The bat is dun with wrinkled wings
   Like fallow article,
And not a song pervades his lips,
   Or none perceptible.

His small umbrella, quaintly halved,
   Describing in the air
An arc alike inscrutable,—
   Elate philosopher!

Deputed from what firmament
   Of what astute abode,
Empowered with what malevolence
   Auspiciously withheld.

To his adroit Creator
   Ascribe no less the praise;
Beneficent, believe me,
   His eccentricities.

The rat is the concisest tenant.
He pays no rent,—
Repudiates the obligation,
On schemes intent.

Balking our wit
To sound or circumvent,
Hate cannot harm
A foe so reticent.

Neither decree
Prohibits him,
Lawful as
Equilibrium.

What mystery pervades a well!
    The water lives so far,
Like neighbor from another world
    Residing in a jar.

The grass does not appear afraid;
    I often wonder he
Can stand so close and look so bold
    At what is dread to me.

Related somehow they may be,—
    The sedge stands next the sea,
Where he is floorless, yet of fear
    No evidence gives he.

But nature is a stranger yet;
    The ones that cite her most
Have never passed her haunted house,
    Nor simplified her ghost.

To pity those that know her not
    Is helped by the regret
That those who know her, know her less
    The nearer her they get.

One of the ones that Midas touched,
Who failed to touch us all,
Was that confiding prodigal,
The reeling oriole.

So drunk, he disavows it
With badinage divine;
So dazzling, we mistake him
For an alighting mine.

A pleader, a dissembler,
An epicure, a thief,—
Betimes an oratorio,
An ecstasy in chief;

The Jesuit of orchards,
He cheats as he enchants
Of an entire attar
For his decamping wants.

The splendor of a Burmah,
The meteor of birds,
Departing like a pageant
Of ballads and of bards.

I never thought that Jason sought
For any golden fleece;
But then I am a rural man,
With thoughts that make for peace.

But if there were a Jason,
Tradition suffer me
Behold his lost aggrandizement
Upon the apple tree.

A route of evanescence
With a revolving wheel;
A resonance of emerald,
A rush of cochineal;
And every blossom on the bush
Adjusts its tumbled head,—
The mail from Tunis, probably,
An easy morning's ride.

How happy is the little stone
That rambles in the road alone,
And doesn't care about careers,
And exigencies never fears;
Whose coat of elemental brown
A passing universe put on;
And independent as the sun,
Associates or glows alone,
Fulfilling absolute decree
In casual simplicity.

No brigadier throughout the year
So civic as the jay.
A neighbor and a warrior too,
With shrill felicity

Pursuing winds that censure us
A February day,
The brother of the universe
Was never blown away.

The snow and he are intimate;
I've often seen them play
When heaven looked upon us all
With such severity,

I felt apology were due
To an insulted sky,
Whose pompous frown was nutriment
To their temerity.

The pillow of this daring head
Is pungent evergreens;
His larder—terse and militant—
Unknown, refreshing things;

His character a tonic,
His future a dispute;
Unfair an immortality
That leaves this neighbor out.

There came a wind like a bugle;
It quivered through the grass,
And a green chill upon the heat
So ominous did pass
We barred the windows and the doors
As from an emerald ghost;
The doom's electric moccasin
That very instant passed.
On a strange mob of panting trees,
And fences fled away,
And rivers where the houses ran
The living looked that day.
The bell within the steeple wild
The flying tidings whirled.
How much can come
And much can go,
And yet abide the world!

High from the earth I heard a bird;
   He trod upon the trees
As he esteemed them trifles,
   And then he spied a breeze,
And situated softly
   Upon a pile of wind
Which in a perturbation
   Nature had left behind.
A joyous-going fellow
   I gathered from his talk,
Which both of benediction
   And badinage partook,
Without apparent burden,
   I learned, in leafy wood
He was the faithful father
   Of a dependent brood;
And this untoward transport
   His remedy for care,—
A contrast to our respites.
   How different we are!

A sloop of amber slips away
   Upon an ether sea,
And wrecks in peace a purple tar,
   The son of ecstasy.

Apparently with no surprise
To any happy flower,
The frost beheads it at its play
In accidental power.
The blond assassin passes on,
The sun proceeds unmoved
To measure off another day
For an approving God.

Not knowing when the dawn will come
    I open every door;
Or has it feathers like a bird,
    Or billows like a shore?

Sweet is the swamp with its secrets,
    Until we meet a snake;
'Tis then we sigh for houses,
    And our departure take
At that enthralling gallop
    That only childhood knows.
A snake is summer's treason,
    And guile is where it goes.

To make a prairie it takes a clover
    and one bee,—
One clover, and a bee,
And revery.
The revery alone will do
If bees are few.

TIME AND ETERNITY

On this wondrous sea,
Sailing silently,
    Ho! pilot, ho!
Knowest thou the shore
Where no breakers roar,
    Where the storm is o'er?

In the silent west
Many sails at rest,
    Their anchors fast;
Thither I pilot thee.—
Land, ho! Eternity!
    Ashore at last!

I never lost as much but twice,
And that was in the sod;
Twice have I stood a beggar
Before the door of God!

Angels, twice descending,
Reimbursed my store.
Burglar, banker, father,
I am poor once more!

There's something quieter than sleep
    Within this inner room!
It wears a sprig upon its breast,
    And will not tell its name.

Some touch it and some kiss it,
    Some chafe its idle hand;
It has a simple gravity
    I do not understand!

While simple-hearted neighbors
    Chat of the "early dead,"
We, prone to periphrasis,
    Remark that birds have fled!

A throe upon the features
A hurry in the breath,
An ecstasy of parting
Denominated "Death,"—

An anguish at the mention,
Which, when to patience grown,
I've known permission given
To rejoin its own.

Exultation is the going
Of an inland soul to sea,—
Past the houses, past the headlands,
Into deep eternity!

Bred as we, among the mountains,
Can the sailor understand
The divine intoxication
Of the first league out from land?

One dignity delays for all,
One mitered afternoon.
None can avoid this purple,
None evade this crown.

Coach it insures, and footmen,
Chamber and state and throng;
Bells, also, in the village,
As we ride grand along.

What dignified attendants,
What service when we pause!
How loyally at parting
Their hundred hats they raise!

How pomp surpassing ermine,
When simple you and I
Present our meek escutcheon,
And claim the rank to die!

Some, too fragile for winter winds,
The thoughtful grave encloses,—
Tenderly tucking them in from frost
Before their feet are cold.

Never the treasures in her nest
The cautious grave exposes,
Building where schoolboy dare not look
And sportsman is not bold.

This covert have all the children
Early aged, and often cold,—
Sparrows unnoticed by the Father;
Lambs for whom time had not a fold.

How many times these low feet staggered,
Only the soldered mouth can tell;
Try! can you stir the awful rivet?
Try! can you lift the hasps of steel?

Stroke the cool forehead, hot so often,
Lift, if you can, the listless hair;
Handle the adamantine fingers
Never a thimble more shall wear.

Buzz the dull flies on the chamber window;
Brave shines the sun through the freckled pane;
Fearless the cobweb swings from the ceiling—
Indolent housewife, in daisies lain!

I shall know why, when time is over,
And I have ceased to wonder why;
Christ will explain each separate anguish
In the fair schoolroom of the sky.

He will tell me what Peter promised,
And I, for wonder at his woe,
I shall forget the drop of anguish
That scalds me now, that scalds me now.

I lost a world the other day.
Has anybody found?
You'll know it by the row of stars
Around its forehead bound.

A rich man might not notice it;
Yet to my frugal eye
Of more esteem than ducats.
Oh, find it, sir, for me!

If I shouldn't be alive
When the robins come,
Give the one in red cravat
A memorial crumb.

If I couldn't thank you,
Being just asleep,
You will know I'm trying
With my granite lip!

I should not dare to leave my friend,
Because—because if he should die
While I was gone, and I—too late—
Should reach the heart that wanted me;

If I should disappoint the eyes
That hunted, hunted so, to see,
And could not bear to shut until
They "noticed" me—they noticed me;

If I should stab the patient faith
So sure I'd come—so sure I'd come,
It listening, listening, went to sleep
Telling my tardy name,—

My heart would wish it broke before,
Since breaking then, since breaking then,
Were useless as next morning's sun,
Where midnight frosts had lain!

On this long storm the rainbow rose,
On this late morn the sun;
The clouds, like listless elephants,
Horizons straggled down.

The birds rose smiling in their nests,
The gales indeed were done;
Alas! how heedless were the eyes
On whom the summer shone!

The quiet nonchalance of death
No daybreak can bestir;
The slow archangel's syllables
Must awaken her.

I like a look of agony,
Because I know it's true;
Men do not sham convulsion,
Nor simulate a throe.

The eyes glaze once, and that is death.
Impossible to feign
The beads upon the forehead
By homely anguish strung.

I breathed enough to learn the trick,
    And now, removed from air,
I simulate the breath so well,
    That one, to be quite sure

The lungs are stirless, must descend
    Among the cunning cells,
And touch the pantomime himself.
    How cool the bellows feels!

Safe in their alabaster chambers,
Untouched by morning and untouched by noon,
Sleep the meek members of the resurrection,
Rafter of satin, and roof of stone.

Light laughs the breeze in her castle above them;
Babbles the bee in a stolid ear;
Pipe the sweet birds in ignorant cadence,—
Ah, what sagacity perished here!

Grand go the years in the crescent above them;
Worlds scoop their arcs, and firmaments row,
Diadems drop and Doges surrender,
Soundless as dots on a disc of snow.

The only ghost I ever saw
Was dressed in mechlin,—so;
He wore no sandal on his foot,
And stepped like flakes of snow.
His gait was soundless, like the bird,
But rapid, like the roe;
His fashions quaint, mosaic,
Or, haply, mistletoe.

His conversation seldom,
His laughter like the breeze
That dies away in dimples
Among the pensive trees.
Our interview was transient,—
Of me, himself was shy;
And God forbid I look behind
Since that appalling day!

Tie the strings to my life, my Lord,
    Then I am ready to go!
Just a look at the horses—
    Rapid! That will do!

Put me in on the firmest side,
    So I shall never fall;
For we must ride to the Judgment,
    And it's partly down hill.

But never I mind the bridges,
    And never I mind the sea;
Held fast in everlasting race
    By my own choice and thee.

Goodbye to the life I used to live,
    And the world I used to know;
And kiss the hills for me, just once;
    Now I am ready to go!

I felt a funeral in my brain,
   And mourners, to and fro,
Kept treading, treading, till it seemed
   That sense was breaking through.

And when they all were seated,
   A service like a drum
Kept beating, beating, till I thought
   My mind was going numb.

And then I heard them lift a box,
   And creak across my soul
With those same boots of lead, again.
   Then space began to toll

As all the heavens were a bell,
   And Being but an ear,
And I and silence some strange race,
   Wrecked, solitary, here.

A clock stopped—not the mantel's;
    Geneva's farthest skill
Can't put the puppet bowing
    That just now dangled still.

An awe came on the trinket!
    The figures hunched with pain,
Then quivered out of decimals
    Into degreeless noon.

It will not stir for doctors,
    This pendulum of snow;
The shopman importunes it,
    While cool, concernless No

Nods from the gilded pointers,
    Nods from the seconds slim,
Decades of arrogance between
    The dial life and him.

It struck me every day
    The lightning was as new
As if the cloud that instant slit
    And let the fire through.

It burned me in the night,
    It blistered in my dream;
It sickened fresh upon my sight
    With every morning's beam.

I thought that storm was brief,—
    The maddest, quickest by;
But Nature lost the date of this,
    And left it in the sky.

I reason, earth is short,
And anguish absolute.
And many hurt;
But what of that?

I reason, we could die:
The best vitality
Cannot excel decay;
But what of that?

I reason that in heaven
Somehow, it will be even,
Some new equation given;
But what of that?

A toad can die of light!
Death is the common right
    Of toads and men,—
Of earl and midge
The privilege.
    Why swagger then?
The gnat's supremacy
Is large as thine.

Death sets a thing significant
The eye had hurried by,
Except a perished creature
Entreat us tenderly

To ponder little workmanships
In crayon or in wool,
With "This was last her fingers did,"
Industrious until

The thimble weighed too heavy,
The stitches stopped themselves,
And then 'twas put among the dust
Upon the closet shelves.

A book I have, a friend gave,
Whose pencil, here and there,
Had notched the place that pleased him,—
At rest his fingers are.

Now, when I read, I read not,
For interrupting tears
Obliterate the etchings
Too costly for repairs.

There's been a death in the opposite house
   As lately as today.
I know it by the numb look
   Such houses have alway.

The neighbors rustle in and out,
   The doctor drives away.
A window opens like a pod,
   Abrupt, mechanically;

Somebody flings a mattress out,—
   The children hurry by;
They wonder if It died on that,—
   I used to when a boy.

The minister goes stiffly in
   As if the house were his,
And he owned all the mourners now,
   And little boys besides;

And then the milliner, and the man
   Of the appalling trade,
To take the measure of the house.
   There'll be that dark parade

Of tassels and of coaches soon;
   It's easy as a sign,—
The intuition of the news
   In just a country town.

No rack can torture me,
My soul's at liberty.
Behind this mortal bone
There knits a bolder one

You cannot prick with saw,
Nor rend with scimitar.
Two bodies therefore be;
Bind one, and one will flee.

The eagle of his nest
No easier divest
And gain the sky,
Than mayest thou,

Except thyself may be
Thine enemy;
Captivity is consciousness,
So's liberty.

They dropped like flakes, they dropped like stars,
    Like petals from a rose,
When suddenly across the June
    A wind with fingers goes.

They perished in the seamless grass,—
    No eye could find the place;
But God on his repealless list
    Can summon every face.

I read my sentence steadily,
Reviewed it with my eyes,
To see that I made no mistake
In its extremest clause,—

The date, and manner of the shame;
And then the pious form
That "God have mercy" on the soul
The jury voted him.

I made my soul familiar
With her extremity,
That at the last it should not be
A novel agony,

But she and Death, acquainted,
Meet tranquilly as friends,
Salute and pass without a hint—
And there the matter ends.

'Twas just this time last year I died.
　I know I heard the corn,
When I was carried by the farms,—
　It had the tassels on.

I thought how yellow it would look
　When Richard went to mill;
And then I wanted to get out,
　But something held my will.

I thought just how red apples wedged
　The stubble's joints between;
And carts went stooping round the fields
　To take the pumpkins in.

I wondered which would miss me least,
　And when Thanksgiving came,
If father'd multiply the plates
　To make an even sum.

And if my stocking hung too high,
　Would it blur the Christmas glee,
That not a Santa Claus could reach
　The altitude of me?

But this sort grieved myself, and so
　I thought how it would be
When just this time, some perfect year,
　Themselves should come to me.

Triumph may be of several kinds.
There's triumph in the room
When that old imperator, Death,
By faith is overcome.

There's triumph of the finer mind
When truth, affronted long,
Advances calm to her supreme,
Her God her only throng.

A triumph when temptation's bribe
Is slowly handed back,
One eye upon the heaven renounced
And one upon the rack.

Severer triumph, by himself
Experienced, who can pass
Acquitted from that naked bar,
Jehovah's countenance!

This world is not conclusion;
    A sequel stands beyond,
Invisible, as music,
    But positive, as sound.
It beckons and it baffles;
    Philosophies don't know,
And through a riddle, at the last,
    Sagacity must go.
To guess it puzzles scholars;
    To gain it, men have shown
Contempt of generations,
    And crucifixion known.

I've seen a dying eye
Run round and round a room
In search of something, as it seemed,
Then cloudier become;
And then, obscure with fog,
And then be soldered down,
Without disclosing what it be,
'Twere blessed to have seen.

I died for beauty, but was scarce
Adjusted in the tomb,
When one who died for truth was lain
In an adjoining room.

He questioned softly why I failed?
"For beauty," I replied.
"And I for truth,—the two are one;
We brethren are," he said.

And so, as kinsmen met a night,
We talked between the rooms,
Until the moss had reached our lips,
And covered up our names.

It was not death, for I stood up,
And all the dead lie down;
It was not night, for all the bells
Put out their tongues, for noon.

It was not frost, for on my flesh
I felt siroccos crawl,—
Nor fire, for just my marble feet
Could keep a chancel cool.

And yet it tasted like them all;
The figures I have seen
Set orderly, for burial,
Reminded me of mine,

As if my life were shaven
And fitted to a frame,
And could not breathe without a key;
And 'twas like midnight, some,
When everything that ticked has stopped,
And space stares, all around,
Or grisly frosts, first autumn morns,
Repeal the beating ground.

But most like chaos,—stopless, cool,—
Without a chance or spar,
Or even a report of land
To justify despair.

I heard a fly buzz when I died;
    The stillness round my form
Was like the stillness in the air
    Between the heaves of storm.

The eyes beside had wrung them dry,
    And breaths were gathering sure
For that last onset, when the king
    Be witnessed in his power.
I willed my keepsakes, signed away
    What portion of me I
Could make assignable,—and then
    There interposed a fly,

With blue, uncertain, stumbling buzz,
    Between the light and me;
And then the windows failed, and then
    I could not see to see.

If I may have it when it's dead
    I will contented be;
If just as soon as breath is out
    It shall belong to me,

Until they lock it in the grave,
    'Tis bliss I cannot weigh,
For though they lock thee in the grave,
    Myself can hold the key.

Think of it, lover! I and thee
    Permitted face to face to be;
After a life, a death we'll say,—
    For death was that, and this is thee.

It was too late for man,
But early yet for God;
Creation impotent to help,
But prayer remained our side.

How excellent the heaven,
When earth cannot be had;
How hospitable, then, the face
Of our old neighbor, God!

Departed to the judgment,
A mighty afternoon;
Great clouds like ushers leaning,
Creation looking on.

The flesh surrendered, canceled,
The bodiless begun;
Two worlds, like audiences, disperse
And leave the soul alone.

There is a shame of nobleness
Confronting sudden pelf,—
A finer shame of ecstasy
Convicted of itself.

A best disgrace a brave man feels,
Acknowledged of the brave,—
One more "Ye Blessed" to be told;
But that's behind the grave.

Afraid? Of whom am I afraid?
Not death; for who is he?
The porter of my father's lodge
As much abasheth me.

Of life? 'Twere odd I fear a thing
That comprehendeth me
In one or more existences
At Deity's decree.

Of resurrection? Is the east
Afraid to trust the morn
With her fastidious forehead?
As soon impeach my crown!

A long, long sleep, a famous sleep
That makes no show for dawn
By stretch of limb or stir of lid,—
An independent one.

Was ever idleness like this?
Within a hut of stone
To bask the centuries away
Nor once look up for noon?

Our journey had advanced;
Our feet were almost come
To that odd fork in Being's road,
Eternity by term.

Our pace took sudden awe,
Our feet reluctant led.
Before were cities, but between,
The forest of the dead.

Retreat was out of hope,—
Behind, a sealed route,
Eternity's white flag before,
And God at every gate.

They say that "time assuages,"—
    Time never did assuage;
An actual suffering strengthens,
    As sinews do, with age.

Time is a test of trouble,
    But not a remedy.
If such it prove, it prove too
    There was no malady.

One need not be a chamber to be haunted,
One need not be a house;
The brain has corridors surpassing
Material place.

Far safer, of a midnight meeting
External ghost,
Than an interior confronting
That whiter host.

Far safer through an abbey gallop,
The stones achase,
Than, moonless, one's own self encounter
In lonesome place.

Ourself, behind ourself concealed,
Should startle most;
Assassin, hid in our apartment,
Be horror's least.

The prudent carries a revolver,
He bolts the door,
O'erlooking a superior specter
More near.

Because I could not stop for Death,
He kindly stopped for me;
The carriage held but just ourselves
And Immortality.

We slowly drove, he knew no haste,
And I had put away
My labor, and my leisure too,
For his civility.

We passed the school where children played,
Their lessons scarcely done;
We passed the fields of gazing grain,
We passed the setting sun.

We paused before a house that seemed
A swelling of the ground;
The roof was scarcely visible,
The cornice but a mound.

Since then 'tis centuries; but each
Feels shorter than the day
I first surmised the horses' heads
Were toward eternity.

We thirst at first,—'tis Nature's act;
    And later, when we die,
A little water supplicate
    Of fingers going by.

It intimates the finer want,
    Whose adequate supply
Is that great water in the west
    Termed immortality.

Essential oils are wrung:
The attar from the rose
Is not expressed by suns alone,
It is the gift of screws.

The general rose decays;
But this, in lady's drawer,
Makes summer when the lady lies
In ceaseless rosemary.

A death-blow is a life-blow to some
Who, till they died, did not alive become;
Who, had they lived, had died, but when
They died, vitality begun.

Ample make this bed.
Make this bed with awe;
In it wait till judgment break
Excellent and fair.

Be its mattress straight,
Be its pillow round;
Let no sunrise' yellow noise
Interrupt this ground.

I sing to use the waiting,
　　My bonnet but to tie,
And shut the door unto my house;
　　No more to do have I,

Till, his best step approaching,
　　We journey to the day,
And tell each other how we sang
　　To keep the dark away.

It is an honorable thought,
　　And makes one lift one's hat,
As one encountered gentlefolk
　　Upon a daily street,

That we've immortal place,
　　Though pyramids decay,
And kingdoms, like the orchard,
　　Flit russetly away.

Death is a dialogue between
The spirit and the dust.
"Dissolve," says Death. The Spirit, "Sir,
I have another trust."

Death doubts it, argues from the ground.
The Spirit turns away,
Just laying off, for evidence,
An overcoat of clay.

The dying need but little, dear,—
　A glass of water's all,
A flower's unobtrusive face
　To punctuate the wall,

A fan, perhaps, a friend's regret,
　And certainly that one
No color in the rainbow
　Perceives when you are gone.

I never saw a moor,
I never saw the sea;
Yet know I how the heather looks,
And what a wave must be.

I never spoke with God,
Nor visited in heaven;
Yet certain am I of the spot
As if the chart were given.

The soul should always stand ajar,
　That if the heaven inquire,
He will not be obliged to wait,
　Or shy of troubling her.

Depart, before the host has slid
　The bolt upon the door,
To seek for the accomplished guest,—
　Her visitor no more.

Let down the bars, O Death!
The tired flocks come in
Whose bleating ceases to repeat,
Whose wandering is done.

Thine is the stillest night,
Thine the securest fold;
Too near thou art for seeking thee,
Too tender to be told.

The bustle in a house
The morning after death
Is solemnest of industries
Enacted upon earth,—

The sweeping up the heart,
And putting love away
We shall not want to use again
Until eternity.

A train went through a burial gate,
A bird broke forth and sang,
And trilled, and quivered, and shook his throat
Till all the churchyard rang;

And then adjusted his little notes,
And bowed and sang again.
Doubtless, he thought it meet of him
To say goodbye to men.

The last night that she lived,
It was a common night,
Except the dying; this to us
Made nature different.

We noticed smallest things,—
Things overlooked before,
By this great light upon our minds
Italicized, as 'twere.

As we went out and in,
Between her final room
And rooms where those to be alive
Tomorrow were, a blame

That others could exist
While she must finish quite,
A jealousy for her arose
So nearly infinite.

We waited while she passed;
It was a narrow time,
Too jostled were our souls to speak,
At length the notice came.

She mentioned, and forgot;
Then lightly as a reed
Bent to the water, struggled scarce,
Consented, and was dead.

And we, we placed the hair,
And drew the head erect;
And then an awful leisure was
Belief to regulate.

My cocoon tightens, colors tease,
I'm feeling for the air;
A dim capacity for wings
Degrades the dress I wear.

A power of butterfly must be
The aptitude to fly,
Meadows of majesty concedes
And easy sweeps of sky.

So I must baffle at the hint
And cipher at the sign,
And make much blunder, if at last
I take the clue divine.

The clouds their backs together laid,
The north begun to push,
The forests galloped till they fell,
The lightning skipped like mice;
The thunder crumbled like a stuff—
How good to be safe in tombs,
Where nature's temper cannot reach,
Nor vengeance ever comes!

Step lightly on this narrow spot!
The broadest land that grows
Is not so ample as the breast
These emerald seams enclose.

Step lofty; for this name is told
As far as cannon dwell,
Or flag subsist, or fame export
Her deathless syllable.

Immortal is an ample word
    When what we need is by,
But when it leaves us for a time,
    'Tis a necessity.

Of heaven above the firmest proof
    We fundamental know,
Except for its marauding hand,
    It had been heaven below.

That short, potential stir
That each can make but once,
That bustle so illustrious
'Tis almost consequence,

Is the *éclat* of death.
Oh, thou unknown renown
That not a beggar would accept,
Had he the power to spurn!

Look back on time with kindly eyes,
He doubtless did his best;
How softly sinks his trembling sun
In human nature's west!

We never know we go,—when we are going
   We jest and shut the door;
Fate following behind us bolts it,
   And we accost no more.

Pompless no life can pass away;
   The lowliest career
To the same pageant wends its way
   As that exalted here.
How cordial is the mystery!
   The hospitable pall
A "this way" beckons spaciously,—
   A miracle for all!

How dare the robins sing,
   When men and women hear
Who since they went to their account
   Have settled with the year!—
Paid all that life had earned
   In one consummate bill,
And now, what life or death can do
   Is immaterial.
Insulting is the sun
   To him whose mortal light,
Beguiled of immortality,
   Bequeaths him to the night.
In deference to him
   Extinct be every hum,
Whose garden wrestles with the dew,
   At daybreak overcome!

Sweet hours have perished here;
   This is a mighty room;
Within its precincts hopes have played,—
   Now shadows in the tomb.

Death is like the insect
   Menacing the tree,
Competent to kill it,
   But decoyed may be.

Bait it with the balsam,
   Seek it with the knife,
Baffle, if it cost you
   Everything in life.

Then, if it have burrowed
   Out of reach of skill,
Ring the tree and leave it,—
   'Tis the vermin's will.

The grave my little cottage is,
   Where, keeping house for thee,
I make my parlor orderly,
   And lay the marble tea,

For two divided, briefly,
   A cycle, it may be,
Till everlasting life unite
   In strong society.

THE SINGLE HOUND

One Sister have I in our house,
And one a hedge away,
There's only one recorded
But both belong to me.

One came the way that I came
And wore my last year's gown,
The other as a bird her nest,
Builded our hearts among.

She did not sing as we did,
It was a different tune,
Herself to her a music
As Bumblebee of June.

Today is far from childhood
But up and down the hills
I held her hand the tighter,
Which shortened all the miles.

And still her hum the years among
Deceives the Butterfly,
Still in her eye the Violets lie
Moldered this many May.

I spilt the dew but took the morn,
I chose this single star
From out the wide night's numbers,
Sue—forevermore!

Adventure most unto itself
The Soul condemned to be;
Attended by a Single Hound—
Its own Identity.

The Soul that has a Guest,
Doth seldom go abroad,
Diviner Crowd at home
Obliterate the need,
And courtesy forbid
A Host's departure, when
Upon Himself be visiting
The Emperor of Men!

Except the smaller size, no Lives are round,
These hurry to a sphere, and show, and end.
The larger, slower grow, and later hang—
The Summers of Hesperides are long.

Fame is a fickle food
Upon a shifting plate,
Whose table once a Guest, but not
The second time, is set.

Whose crumbs the crows inspect,
And with ironic caw
Flap past it to the Farmer's corn;
Men eat of it and die.

The right to perish might be thought
An undisputed right,
Attempt it, and the Universe upon the opposite
Will concentrate its officers—
You cannot even die,
But Nature and Mankind must pause
To pay you scrutiny.

Peril as a possession
'Tis good to bear,
Danger disintegrates satiety;
There's Basis there
Begets an awe,
That searches Human Nature's creases
As clean as Fire.

When Etna basks and purrs,
Naples is more afraid
Than when she shows her Garnet Tooth;
Security is loud.

Reverse cannot befall that fine Prosperity
Whose sources are interior
As soon Adversity
A diamond overtake,
In far Bolivian ground;
Misfortune hath no implement
Could mar it, if it found.

To be alive is power,
Existence in itself,
Without a further function,
Omnipotence enough.

To be alive and Will—
'Tis able as a God!
The Further of ourselves be what—
Such being Finitude?

Witchcraft has not a pedigree,
'Tis early as our breath,
And mourners meet it going out
The moment of our death.

Exhilaration is the Breeze
That lifts us from the ground,
And leaves us in another place
Whose statement is not found;

Returns us not, but after time
We soberly descend,
A little newer for the term
Upon enchanted ground.

No romance sold unto,
Could so enthrall a man
As the perusal of
His individual one.

'Tis fiction's to dilute
To plausibility
Our novel, when 'tis small enough
To credit,—'tisn't true!

If what we could were what we would—
Criterion be small;
It is the Ultimate of talk
The impotence to tell.

Perception of an
Object costs
Precise the Object's loss.
Perception in itself a gain
Replying to its price;
The Object Absolute is nought,
Perception sets it fair,
And then upbraids a Perfectness
That situates so far.

No other can reduce
Our mortal consequence,
Like the remembering it be nought
A period from hence.
But contemplation for
Contemporaneous nought
Our single competition;
Jehovah's estimate.

The blunder is to estimate,—
"Eternity is *Then*,"
We say, as of a station.
Meanwhile he is so near,
He joins me in my ramble,
Divides abode with me,
No friend have I that so persists
As this Eternity.

My Wheel is in the dark,—
I cannot see a spoke,
Yet know its dripping feet
Go round and round.

My foot is on the tide—
An unfrequented road,
Yet have all roads
A "clearing" at the end.

Some have resigned the loom,
Some in the busy tomb
Find quaint employ,
Some with new, stately feet
Pass royal through the gate,
Flinging the problem back at you and me.

There is another Loneliness
That many die without,
Not want or friend occasions it,
Or circumstance or lot.

But nature sometimes, sometimes thought,
And whoso it befall
Is richer than could be divulged
By mortal numeral.

So gay a flower bereaved the mind
As if it were a woe,
Is Beauty an affliction, then?
Tradition ought to know.

Glory is that bright tragic thing,
That for an instant
Means Dominion,
Warms some poor name
That never felt the sun,
Gently replacing
In oblivion.

The missing All prevented me
From missing minor things.
If nothing larger than a World's
Departure from a hinge,
Or Sun's extinction be observed,
'Twas not so large that I
Could lift my forehead from my work
For curiosity.

His mind, of man a secret makes,
I meet him with a start,
He carries a circumference
In which I have no part,
Or even if I deem I do—
He otherwise may know.
Impregnable to inquest,
However neighborly.

The suburbs of a secret
A strategist should keep,
Better than on a dream intrude
To scrutinize the sleep.

The difference between despair
And fear, is like the one
Between the instant of a wreck,
And when the wreck has been.

The mind is smooth,—no motion—
Contented as the eye
Upon the forehead of a Bust,
That knows it cannot see.

There is a solitude of space,
A solitude of sea,
A solitude of death, but these
Society shall be,
Compared with that profounder site.
That polar privacy,
A Soul admitted to Itself:
Finite Infinity.

The props assist the house
Until the house is built,
And then the props withdraw—
And adequate, erect,
The house supports itself;
Ceasing to recollect
The auger and the carpenter.
Just such a retrospect
Hath the perfected life,
A past of plank and nail,
And slowness,—then the scaffolds drop—
Affirming it a soul.

The gleam of an heroic act,
Such strange illumination—
The Possible's slow fuse is lit
By the Imagination!

To disappear enhances;
The man who runs away
Is tinctured for an instant
With Immortality.

But yesterday a vagrant,
Today in memory lain
With superstitious merit
We tamper with again.

But never far as Honor
Removes the paltry One,
And impotent to cherish
We hasten to adorn.

Of Death the sharpest function,
That, just as we discern,
The Excellence defies us;
Securest gathered then

The fruit perverse to plucking,
But leaning to the sight
With the ecstatic limit
Of unobtained Delight.

Down Time's quaint stream
Without an oar,
We are enforced to sail,
Our Port—a secret—
Our Perchance—a gale.
What Skipper would
Incur the risk,
What Buccaneer would ride,
Without a surety from the wind
Or schedule of the tide?

I bet with every Wind that blew
Till Nature in chagrin
Employed a Fact to visit me
And scuttle my Balloon.

The Future never spoke,
Nor will he, like the Dumb,
Reveal by sign or syllable
Of his profound To Come.
But when the news be ripe,
Presents it in the Act—
Forestalling preparation
Escape or substitute.
Indifferent to him
The Dower as the Doom,
His office but to execute
Fate's Telegram to him.

Two lengths has every day,
Its absolute extent—
And area superior
By hope or heaven lent.
Eternity will be
Velocity, or pause,
At fundamental signals
From fundamental laws.
To die, is not to go—
On doom's consummate chart
No territory new is staked,
Remain thou as thou art.

The Soul's superior instants
Occur to Her alone,
When friend and earth's occasion
Have infinite withdrawn.

Or she, Herself, ascended
To too remote a height,
For lower recognition
Than Her Omnipotent.

This mortal abolition
Is seldom, but as fair
As Apparition, subject
To autocratic air.

Eternity's disclosure
To favorites, a few,
Of the Colossal substance
Of immortality.

Nature is what we see,
The Hill, the Afternoon—
Squirrel, Eclipse, the Bumblebee,
Nay—Nature is Heaven.

Nature is what we hear,
The Bobolink, the Sea—
Thunder, the Cricket—
Nay,—Nature is Harmony.

Nature is what we know
But have no art to say,
So impotent our wisdom is
To Her simplicity.

Ah, Teneriffe!
Receding Mountain!
Purple of Ages pause for you,
Sunset reviews her Sapphire Regiment,
Day drops you her red Adieu!
Still, clad in your mail of ices,
Thigh of granite and thew of steel—
Heedless, alike, of pomp or parting,
Ah, Teneriffe!
I'm kneeling still.

"Morning" means "Milking" to the Farmer
Dawn to the Teneriffe—
Dice to the Maid.
"Morning" means just Risk to the Lover—
Just Revelation to the Beloved.

Epicures date a breakfast by it!
Brides, an Apocalypse,
Worlds, a flood,
Faint-going lives, their lapse from sighing,
Faith, the Experiment of our Lord!

She died at play,
Gamboled away
Her lease of spotted hours,
Then sank as gaily as a Turk
Upon a couch of flowers.

Her ghost strolled softly o'er the hill
Yesterday and today,
Her vestments as the silver fleece,
Her countenance as spray.

A little madness in the Spring
Is wholesome even for the King,
But God be with the Clown,
Who ponders this tremendous scene—
This whole experiment of green,
As if it were his own!

I can't tell you, but you feel it—
Nor can you tell me,
Saints with vanished slate and pencil
Solve our April day.

Sweeter than a vanished Frolic
From a vanished Green!
Swifter than the hoofs of Horsemen
Round a ledge of Dream!

Modest, let us walk among it,
With our "faces veiled,"
As they say polite Archangels
Do, in meeting God.

Not for *me* to prate about it,
Not for *you* to say
To some fashionable Lady—
"Charming April Day!"

Rather Heaven's "Peter Parley"
By which, Children—slow—
To sublimer recitations
Are prepared to go!

Some Days retired from the rest
In soft distinction lie,
The Day that a companion came—
Or was obliged to die.

Like Men and Women shadows walk
Upon the hills today,
With here and there a mighty bow,
Or trailing courtesy
To Neighbors, doubtless, of their own;
Not quickened to perceive
Minuter landscape, as Ourselves
And Boroughs where we live.

The butterfly obtains
But little sympathy,
Though favorably mentioned
In Entomology.
Because he travels freely
And wears a proper coat,
The circumspect are certain
That he is dissolute.
Had he the homely scutcheon of modest Industry,
'Twere fitter certifying for Immortality.

Beauty crowds me till I die,
Beauty, mercy have on me!
But if I expire today,
Let it be in sight of thee.

We spy the Forests and the Hills
The tents to Nature's Show,
Mistake the outside for the in
And mention what we saw.

Could Commentators on the sign
Of Nature's Caravan
Obtain "admission," as a child,
Some Wednesday afternoon?

I never told the buried gold
Upon the hill that lies,
I saw the sun, his plunder done,
Crouch low to guard his prize.

He stood as near, as stood you here,
A pace had been between—
Did but a snake bisect the brake,
My life had forfeit been.

That was a wondrous booty,
I hope 'twas honest gained—
Those were the finest ingots
That ever kissed the spade.

Whether to keep the secret—
Whether to reveal—
Whether, while I ponder
Kidd may sudden sail—

Could a Shrewd advise me
We might e'en divide—
Should a Shrewd betray me—
"Atropos" decide!

The largest fire ever known
Occurs each afternoon,
Discovered is without surprise,
Proceeds without concern:
Consumes, and no report to men,
An Occidental town,
Rebuilt another morning
To be again burned down.

Bloom upon the Mountain, stated,
Blameless of a name.
Efflorescence of a Sunset—
Reproduced, the same.

Seed, had I, my purple sowing
Should endow the Day,
Not a tropic of the twilight
Show itself away.

Who for tilling, to the Mountain
Come, and disappear—
Whose be Her renown, or fading,
Witness, is not here.

While I state—the solemn petals
Far as North and East,
Far as South and West expanding,
Culminate in rest.

And the Mountain to the Evening
Fit His countenance,
Indicating by no muscle
The Experience.

March is the month of expectation,
The things we do not know.
The Persons of prognostication
Are coming now.
We try to sham becoming firmness,
But pompous joy
Betrays us, as his first betrothal
Betrays a boy.

The Duties of the Wind are few—
To cast the Ships at sea,
Establish March,
The Floods escort,
And usher Liberty.

The Winds drew off
Like hungry dogs
Defeated of a bone.
Through fissures in
Volcanic cloud
The yellow lightning shown.
The trees held up
Their mangled limbs
Like animals in pain,
When Nature falls
Upon herself,
Beware an Austrian!

I think that the root of the Wind is Water,
It would not sound so deep
Were it a firmamental product,
Airs no Oceans keep—
Mediterranean intonations,
To a Current's ear
There is a maritime conviction
In the atmosphere.

So, from the mold,
Scarlet and gold
Many a Bulb will rise,
Hidden away cunningly
From sagacious eyes.
So, from cocoon
Many a Worm
Leap so Highland gay,
Peasants like me—
Peasants like thee,
Gaze perplexedly.

The long sigh of the Frog
Upon a Summer's day,
Enacts intoxication
Upon the revery.
But his receding swell
Substantiates a peace,
That makes the ear inordinate
For corporal release.

A cap of lead across the sky
Was tight and surly drawn,
We could not find the Mighty Face,
The figure was withdrawn.

A chill came up as from a shaft,
Our noon became a well,
A thunder storm combines the charms
Of Winter and of Hell.

(Sent with brilliant flowers.)

I send two Sunsets—
Day and I in competition ran,
I finished two, and several stars,
While He was making one.

His own is ampler—
But, as I was saying to a friend,
Mine is the more convenient
To carry in the hand.

Of this is Day composed
A morning and a noon,
A Revelry unspeakable
And then a gay Unknown;
Whose Pomps allure and spurn
And dower and deprive,
And penury for glory
Remedilessly leave.

The Hills erect their purple heads,
The Rivers lean to see—
Yet Man has not, of all the throng,
A curiosity.

Lightly stepped a yellow star
To its lofty place,
Loosed the Moon her silver hat
From her lustral face.
All of evening softly lit
As an astral hall—
"Father," I observed to Heaven,
"You are punctual."

The Moon upon her fluent route
Defiant of a road,
The stars Etruscan argument,
Substantiate a God.
If Aims impel these Astral Ones,
The Ones allowed to know,
Know that which makes them as forgot
As Dawn forgets them now.

Like some old-fashioned miracle
When Summertime is done,
Seems Summer's recollection
And the affairs of June.

As infinite tradition
As Cinderella's bays,
Or Little John of Lincoln Green,
Or Bluebeard's galleries.

Her Bees have a fictitious hum,
Her Blossoms, like a dream,
Elate us until we almost weep
So plausible they seem.

Her Memories like strains review—
When Orchestra is dumb,
The Violin in baize replaced
And Ear and Heaven numb.

Glowing is her Bonnet,
Glowing is her Cheek,
Glowing is her Kirtle,
Yet she cannot speak!

Better, as the Daisy
From the Summer hill,
Vanish unrecorded
Save by tearful Rill,

Save by loving Sunrise
Looking for her face,
Save by feet unnumbered
Pausing at the place!

Forever cherished be the tree,
Whose apple Winter warm,
Enticed to breakfast from the sky
Two Gabriels yestermorn;

They registered in Nature's book
As Robin—Sire and Son,
But angels have that modest way
To screen them from renown.

The Ones that disappeared are back,
The Phoebe and the Crow,
Precisely as in March is heard
The curtness of the Jay—
Be this an Autumn or a Spring?
My wisdom loses way,
One side of me the nuts are ripe—
The other side is May.

Those final Creatures,—who they are—
That, faithful to the close,
Administer her ecstasy,
But just the Summer knows.

Summer begins to have the look,
Peruser of enchanting Book
Reluctantly, but sure, perceives—
A gain upon the backward leaves.

Autumn begins to be inferred
By millinery of the cloud,
Or deeper color in the shawl
That wraps the everlasting hill.

The eye begins its avarice,
A meditation chastens speech,
Some Dyer of a distant tree
Resumes his gaudy industry.

Conclusion is the course of all,
Almost to be perennial,
And then elude stability
Recalls to immortality.

A prompt, executive Bird is the Jay,
Bold as a Bailiff's hymn,
Brittle and brief in quality—
Warrant in every line;
Sitting a bough like a Brigadier,
Confident and straight,
Much is the mien
Of him in March
As a Magistrate.

Like brooms of steel
The Snow and Wind
Had swept the Winter Street,
The House was hooked,
The Sun sent out
Faint Deputies of heat—
Where rode the Bird
The Silence tied
His ample, plodding Steed,
The Apple in the cellar snug
Was all the one that played.

These are the days that Reindeer love
And pranks the Northern star,
This is the Sun's objective
And Finland of the year.

Follow wise Orion
Till you lose your eye,
Dazzlingly decamping
He is just as high.

In winter, in my room,
I came upon a worm,
Pink, lank, and warm.
But as he was a worm
And worms presume,
Not quite with him at home—
Secured him by a string
To something neighboring,
And went along.

A trifle afterward
A thing occurred,
I'd not believe it if I heard—
But state with creeping blood;
A snake, with mottles rare,
Surveyed my chamber floor,
In feature as the worm before,
But ringed with power.
The very string
With which I tied him, too,
When he was mean and new,
That string was there.

I shrank—"How fair you are!"
Propitiation's claw—
"Afraid," he hissed,
"Of me?"
"No cordiality?"
He fathomed me.
Then, to a rhythm slim
Secreted in his form,
As patterns swim,
Projected him.

That time I flew,
Both eyes his way,
Lest he pursue—
Nor ever ceased to run,
Till, in a distant town,
Towns on from mine—
I sat me down;
This was a dream.

Not any sunny tone
From any fervent zone
Finds entrance there.
Better a grave of Balm
Toward human nature's home,
And Robins near,
Than a stupendous Tomb
Proclaiming to the gloom
How dead we are.

For Death,—or rather
For the things 'twill buy,
These put away
Life's opportunity.
The things that Death will buy
Are Room,—Escape
From Circumstances,
And a Name.
How gifts of Life
With Death's gifts may compare,
We know not—
For the rates stop Here.

Dropped into the
Ether Acre!
Wearing the sod gown—
Bonnet of Everlasting laces—
Brooch frozen on!
Horses of blonde—
And coach of silver,
Baggage a strapped Pearl!
Journey of Down
And whip of Diamond—
Riding to meet the Earl!

This quiet Dust was Gentlemen and Ladies,
        And Lads and Girls;
Was laughter and ability and sighing,
        And frocks and curls.
This passive place a Summer's nimble mansion,
        Where Bloom and Bees
Fulfilled their Oriental Circuit,
        Then ceased like these.

'Twas comfort in her dying room
To hear the living clock,
A short relief to have the wind
Walk boldly up and knock,
Diversion from the dying theme
To hear the children play,
But wrong, the mere
That these could live,—
And This of ours must die!

Too cold is this
To warm with sun,
Too stiff to bended be,
To joint this agate were a feat
Outstaring masonry.
How went the agile kernel out—
Contusion of the husk,
Nor rip, nor wrinkle indicate,—
But just an Asterisk.

I watched her face to see which way
She took the awful news,
Whether she died before she heard—
Or in protracted bruise
Remained a few short years with us,
Each heavier than the last—
A further afternoon to fail,
As Flower at fall of Frost.

Today or this noon
She dwelt so close,
I almost touched her;
Tonight she lies
Past neighborhood—
And bough and steeple—
Now past surmise.

I see thee better in the dark,
I do not need a light.
The love of thee a prism be
Excelling violet.

I see thee better for the years
That hunch themselves between,
The miner's lamp sufficient be
To nullify the mine.

And in the grave I see thee best—
Its little panels be
Aglow, all ruddy with the light
I held so high for thee!

What need of day to those whose dark
Hath so surpassing sun,
It deem it be continually
At the meridian?

Low at my problem bending,
Another problem comes,
Larger than mine, serene,
Involving statelier sums;

I check my busy pencil,
My ciphers slip away,
Wherefore, my baffled fingers,
Time Eternity?

If pain for peace prepares,
Lo the "Augustan" years
Our feet await!

If Springs from Winter rise,
Can the Anemone's
Be reckoned up?

If night stands first, then noon,
To gird us for the sun,
What gaze—

When, from a thousand skies,
On our developed eyes
Noons blaze!

I fit for them,
I seek the dark till I am thorough fit.
The labor is a solemn one,
With this sufficient sweet—
That abstinence as mine produce
A purer good for them,
If I succeed,—
If not, I had
The transport of the Aim.

Not one by Heaven defrauded stay,
Although He seem to steal,
He restitutes in some sweet way
Secreted in His will.

The feet of people walking home
In gayer sandals go,
The Crocus, till she rises,
The Vassal of the Snow—
The lips of Hallelujah!
Long years of practice bore,
Till bye and bye these Bargemen
Walked singing on the shore.

Pearls are the Diver's farthings
Extorted from the Sea,
Pinions the Seraph's wagon,
Pedestrians once, as we—
Night is the morning's canvas,
Larceny, legacy,
Death but our rapt attention
To immortality.

My figures fail to tell me
How far the village lies,
Whose Peasants are the angels,
Whose Cantons dot the skies,
My Classics veil their faces,
My Faith that dark adores,
Which from its solemn Abbeys
Such resurrection pours!

We should not mind so small a flower,
Except it quiet bring
Our little garden that we lost
Back to the lawn again.
So spicy her Carnations red,
So drunken reel her Bees,
So silver steal a hundred Flutes
From out a hundred trees,
That whoso sees this little flower,
By faith may clear behold
The Bobolinks around the throne,
And Dandelions gold.

To the staunch Dust we safe commit thee;
Tongue if it hath, inviolate to thee—
Silence denote and Sanctity enforce thee,
Passenger of Infinity!

(Written after the death of Mrs. Browning in 1861.)

Her "Last Poems"—
Poets ended,
Silver perished with her tongue,
Not on record bubbled other
Flute, or Woman, so divine;
Not unto its Summer morning
Robin uttered half the tune—
Gushed too free for the adoring,
From the Anglo-Florentine.
Late the praise—
'Tis dull conferring
On a Head too high to crown,
Diadem or Ducal showing,
Be its Grave sufficient sign.
Yet if we, no Poet's kinsman,
Suffocate with easy woe,
What and if ourself a Bridegroom,
Put Her down, in Italy?

Immured in Heaven! What a Cell!
Let every bondage be,
Thou Sweetest of the Universe,
Like that which ravished thee!

I'm thinking on that other morn,
When Cerements let go,
And Creatures clad in Victory
Go up by two and two!

The overtakelessness of those
Who have accomplished Death,
Majestic is to me beyond
The majesties of Earth.

The soul her "not at Home"
Inscribes upon the flesh,
And takes her fair aerial gait
Beyond the hope of touch.

The Look of Thee, what is it like?
Hast thou a hand or foot,
Or mansion of Identity,
And what is thy Pursuit?

Thy fellows,—are they Realms or Themes?
Hast thou Delight or Fear
Or Longing,—and is that for us
Or values more severe?

Let change transfuse all other traits,
Enact all other blame,
But deign this least certificate—
That thou shalt be the same.

The Devil, had he fidelity,
Would be the finest friend—
Because he has ability,
But Devils cannot mend.
Perfidy is the virtue
That would he but resign,—
The Devil, so amended,
Were durably divine.

Papa above!
Regard a Mouse
O'erpowered by the Cat;
Reserve within thy Kingdom
A "mansion" for the Rat!

Snug in seraphic cupboards
To nibble all the day,
While unsuspecting cycles
Wheel pompously away.

Not when we know
The Power accosts,
The garment of Surprise
Was all our timid Mother wore
At Home, in Paradise.

Elijah's wagon knew no thill,
Was innocent of wheel,
Elijah's horses as unique
As was his vehicle.

Elijah's journey to portray,
Expire with him the skill,
Who justified Elijah,
In feats inscrutable.

"Remember me," implored the Thief—
Oh magnanimity!
"My Visitor in Paradise
I give thee Guaranty."

That courtesy will fair remain,
When the delight is dust,
With which we cite this mightiest case
Of compensated Trust.

Of All, we are allowed to hope,
But Affidavit stands
That this was due, where some, we fear,
Are unexpected friends.

To this apartment deep
No ribaldry may creep;
Untroubled this abode
By any man but God.

"Sown in dishonor?"
Ah! Indeed!
May this dishonor be?
If I were half so fine myself,
I'd notice nobody!

"Sown in corruption?"
By no means!
Apostle is askew;
Corinthians 1:15, narrates
A circumstance or two!

Through lane it lay, through bramble,
Through clearing and through wood,
Banditti often passed us
Upon the lonely road.

The wolf came purring curious,
The owl looked puzzled down,
The serpent's satin figure
Glid stealthily along.

The tempest touched our garments,
The lightning's poignards gleamed,
Fierce from the crag above us
The hungry vulture screamed.

The satyr's fingers beckoned,
The valley murmured "Come"—
These were the mates—and this the road
Those children fluttered home.

Who is it seeks my pillow nights?
With plain inspecting face,
"Did you, or did you not?" to ask,
'Tis Conscience, childhood's nurse.

With martial hand she strokes the hair
Upon my wincing head,
"All rogues shall have their part in"—
What—
            The Phosphorus of God.

His Cheek is his Biographer—
As long as he can blush,
Perdition is Opprobrium;
Past that, he sins in peace.
                            Thief

"Heavenly Father," take to Thee
The supreme iniquity,
Fashioned by Thy candid hand
In a moment contraband.

Though to trust us seem to us
More respectful—"we are dust."
We apologize to Thee
For Thine own Duplicity.

The sweets of Pillage can be known
To no one but the Thief,
Compassion for Integrity
Is his divinest Grief.

The Bible is an antique volume
Written by faded men,
At the suggestion of Holy Specters—
Subjects—Bethlehem—
Eden—the ancient Homestead—
Satan—the Brigadier,
Judas—the great Defaulter,
David—the Troubadour.
Sin—a distinguished Precipice

Others must resist,
Boys that "believe"
Are very lonesome—
Other boys are "lost."
Had but the tale a warbling Teller
All the boys would come—
Orpheus' sermon captivated,
It did not condemn.

A little over Jordan,
As Genesis record,
An Angel and a Wrestler
Did wrestle long and hard.

Till, morning touching mountain,
And Jacob waxing strong,
The Angel begged permission
To breakfast and return.

"Not so," quoth wily Jacob,
And girt his loins anew,
"Until thou bless me, stranger!"
The which acceded to:

Light swung the silver fleeces
Peniel hills among,
And the astonished Wrestler
Found he had worsted God!

Ambition cannot find him,
Affection doesn't know
How many leagues of Nowhere
Lie between them now.
Yesterday undistinguished—
Eminent today,
For our mutual honor—
Immortality!

Dust is the only secret,
Death the only one
You cannot find out all about
In his native town:
Nobody knew his father,
Never was a boy,
Hadn't any playmates
Or early history.

Industrious, laconic,
Punctual, sedate,
Bolder than a Brigand,
Swifter than a Fleet.
Builds like a bird too,
Christ robs the nest—
Robin after robin
Smuggled to rest!

Eden is that old-fashioned House
We dwell in every day,
Without suspecting our abode
Until we drive away.
How fair, on looking back, the Day
We sauntered from the door,
Unconscious our returning
Discover it no more.

Candor, my tepid Friend,
Come not to play with me
The Myrrhs and Mochas of the Mind
Are its Iniquity.

Speech is a symptom of affection,
And Silence one,
The perfectest communication
Is heard of none—
Exists and its endorsement
Is had within—
Behold! said the Apostle,
Yet had not seen.

Who were "the Father and the Son"
We pondered when a child,
And what had they to do with us—
And when portentous told
With inference appalling,
By Childhood fortified,
We thought, "at least they are no worse
Than they have been described."

Who are "the Father and the Son"—
Did we demand today,
"The Father and the Son" himself
Would doubtless specify,
But had they the felicity
When we desired to know,
We better Friends had been, perhaps,
Than time ensue to be.

We start, to learn that we believe
But once, entirely—
Belief, it does not fit so well
When altered frequently.
We blush, that Heaven if we achieve,
Event ineffable—
We shall have shunned, until ashamed
To own the Miracle.

That Love is all there is,
Is all we know of Love;
It is enough, the freight should be
Proportioned to the groove.

The luxury to apprehend
The luxury 'twould be
To look at thee a single time,
An Epicure of me,
In whatsoever Presence, makes,
Till, for a further food
I scarcely recollect to starve,
So first am I supplied.
The luxury to meditate
The luxury it was
To banquet on thy Countenance,
A sumptuousness supplies
To plainer days,
Whose table, far as
Certainty can see,
Is laden with a single crumb—
The consciousness of Thee.

The Sea said "Come" to the Brook,
The Brook said "Let me grow!"
The Sea said "Then you will be a Sea—
I want a brook, Come now!"

All I may, if small,
Do it not display
Larger for its Totalness?
'Tis economy
To bestow a world
And withhold a star,
Utmost is munificence;
Less, though larger, Poor.

Love reckons by itself alone,
"As large as I" relate the Sun
To one who never felt it blaze,
Itself is all the like it has.

The inundation of the Spring
Submerges every soul,
It sweeps the tenement away
But leaves the water whole.
In which the Soul, at first alarmed,
Seeks furtive for its shore,
But acclimated, gropes no more
For that Peninsular.

No Autumn's intercepting chill
Appalls this Tropic Breast,
But African exuberance
And Asiatic Rest.

Volcanoes be in Sicily
And South America,
I judge from my geography.
Volcanoes nearer here,
A lava step, at any time,
Am I inclined to climb,
A crater I may contemplate,
Vesuvius at home.

Distance is not the realm of Fox,
Nor by relay as Bird;
Abated, Distance is until
Thyself, Beloved!

The treason of an accent
Might vilify the Joy—
To breathe,—corrode the rapture
Of Sanctity to be.

How destitute is he
Whose Gold is firm,
Who finds it every time,
The small stale sum—
When Love, with but a pence
Will so display,
As is a disrespect to India!

Crisis is sweet and, set of Heart
Upon the hither side,
Has dowers of prospective
Surrendered by the Tried.
Inquire of the closing Rose
Which Rapture she preferred,
And she will tell you, sighing,
The transport of the Bud.

To tell the beauty would decrease,
To state the Spell demean,
There is a syllableless sea
Of which it is the sign.

My will endeavors for its word
And fails, but entertains
A rapture as of legacies—
Of introspective mines.

To love thee, year by year,
May less appear
Than sacrifice and cease.
However, Dear,
Forever might be short
I thought, to show,
And so I pieced it with a flower now.

I showed her heights she never saw—
"Wouldst climb?" I said,
She said "Not so"—
"With me?" I said, "With me?"
I showed her secrets
Morning's nest,
The rope that Nights were put across—
And now, "Wouldst have me for a Guest?"
She could not find her yes—
And then, I brake my life, and Lo!
A light for her, did solemn glow,
The larger, as her face withdrew—
And could she, further, "No?"

On my volcano grows the grass,—
A meditative spot,
An area for a bird to choose
Would be the general thought.

How red the fire reeks below,
How insecure the sod—
Did I disclose, would populate
With awe my solitude.

If I could tell how glad I was,
I should not be so glad,
But when I cannot make the Force
Nor mold it into word,
I know it is a sign
That new Dilemma be
From mathematics further off,
Than from Eternity.

Her Grace is all she has,
And that, so vast displays,
One Art, to recognize, must be,
Another Art to praise.

No matter where the Saints abide,
They make their circuit fair;
Behold how great a Firmament
Accompanies a star!

To see her is a picture,
To hear her is a tune,
To know her an intemperance
As innocent as June;
By which to be undone
Is dearer than Redemption—
Which never to receive,
Makes mockery of melody
It might have been to live.

So set its sun in thee,
What day is dark to me—
What distance far,
So I the ships may see
That touch how seldomly
Thy shore?

Had this one day not been,
Or could it cease to be—
How smitten, how superfluous
Were every other day!

Lest Love should value less
What Loss would value more,
Had it the stricken privilege—
It cherishes before.

That she forgot me was the least,
I felt it second pain,
That I was worthy to forget
What most I thought upon.

Faithful, was all that I could boast,
But Constancy became,
To her, by her innominate,
A something like a shame.

The incidents of Love
Are more than its Events,
Investments' best expositor
Is the minute per cents.

A little overflowing word
That any hearing had inferred
For ardor or for tears,
Though generations pass away,
Traditions ripen and decay,
As eloquent appears.

Just so, Jesus raps—He does not weary—
Last at the knocker and first at the bell,
Then on divinest tiptoe standing
Might He out-spy the hiding soul.
When He retires, chilled and weary—
It will be ample time for me;
Patient, upon the steps, until then—
Heart, I am knocking low at Thee!

Safe Despair it is that raves,
Agony is frugal,
Puts itself severe away
For its own perusal.

Garrisoned no Soul can be
In the front of Trouble,
Love is one, not aggregate,
Nor is Dying double.

The Face we choose to miss,
Be it but for a day—
As absent as a hundred years
When it has rode away.

Of so divine a loss
We enter but the gain,
Indemnity for loneliness
That such a bliss has been.

The healed Heart shows its shallow scar
With confidential moan,
Not mended by Mortality
Are fabrics truly torn.
To go its convalescent way
So shameless is to see,
More genuine were Perfidy
Than such Fidelity.

Give little anguish
Lives will fret.
Give avalanches—
And they'll slant.
Straighten, look cautious for their breath,
But make no syllable—
Like Death,
    Who only shows his
    Marble disc—
Sublimer sort than speech.

To pile like Thunder to its close,
Then crumble grand away,
While everything created hid—
This would be Poetry:
Or Love,—the two coeval came—
We both and neither prove,
Experience either, and consume—
For none see God and live.

The Stars are old, that stood for me—
The West a little worn,
Yet newer glows the only Gold
I ever cared to earn—
Presuming on that lone result
Her infinite disdain,
But vanquished her with my defeat,
'Twas Victory was slain.

All circumstances are the frame
In which His Face is set,
All Latitudes exist for His
Sufficient continent.

The light His Action and the dark
The Leisure of His Will,
In Him Existence serve, or set
A force illegible.

I did not reach thee,
But my feet slip nearer every day;
Three Rivers and a Hill to cross,
One Desert and a Sea—
I shall not count the journey one
When I am telling thee.

Two deserts—but the year is cold
So that will help the sand—
One desert crossed, the second one
Will feel as cool as land.
Sahara is too little price
To pay for thy Right hand!

The sea comes last. Step merry, feet!
So short have we to go
To play together we are prone,
But we must labor now,
The last shall be the lightest load
That we have had to draw.

The Sun goes crooked—that is night—
Before he makes the bend
We must have passed the middle sea,
Almost we wish the end
Were further off—too great it seems
So near the Whole to stand.

We step like plush, we stand like snow—
The waters murmur now,
Three rivers and the hill are passed,
Two deserts and the sea!
Now Death usurps my premium
And gets the look at Thee.

Index of First Lines

AMERICAN LITERATURE

Little Women — Louisa May Alcott
The Last of the Mohicans — James Fenimore Cooper
The Red Badge of Courage and *Maggie* — Stephen Crane
Selected Poems — Emily Dickinson
Narrative of the Life and Other Writings — Frederick Douglass
The Scarlet Letter — Nathaniel Hawthorne
The Call of the Wild and *White Fang* – Jack London
Moby-Dick — Herman Melville
Major Tales and Poems — Edgar Allan Poe
The Jungle — Upton Sinclair
Uncle Tom's Cabin — Harriet Beecher Stowe
Walden and *Civil Disobedience* — Henry David Thoreau
Adventures of Huckleberry Finn — Mark Twain
The Complete Adventures of Tom Sawyer — Mark Twain
Ethan Frome and *Summer* — Edith Wharton
Leaves of Grass — Walt Whitman

WORLD LITERATURE

Tales from the 1001 Nights — Sir Richard Burton
Don Quixote — Miguel de Cervantes
The Divine Comedy — Dante Alighieri
Crime and Punishment — Fyodor Dostoevsky
The Count of Monte Cristo — Alexandre Dumas
The Three Musketeers — Alexandre Dumas
Selected Tales — Jacob and Wilhelm Grimm
The Iliad — Homer
The Odyssey — Homer
The Hunchback of Notre-Dame — Victor Hugo
Les Misérables — Victor Hugo
The Metamorphosis and *The Trial* — Franz Kafka
The Phantom of the Opera — Gaston Leroux
The Prince — Niccolò Machiavelli
The Art of War — Sun Tzu
The Death of Ivan Ilych and Other Stories — Leo Tolstoy
Around the World in Eighty Days — Jules Verne
Candide and *The Maid of Orléans* — Voltaire
The Bhagavad Gita — Vyasa

BRITISH LITERATURE

Beowulf — Anonymous
Emma — Jane Austen
Persuasion — Jane Austen
Pride and Prejudice — Jane Austen
Sense and Sensibility — Jane Austen
Peter Pan — J. M. Barrie
Jane Eyre — Charlotte Brontë
Wuthering Heights — Emily Brontë
Alice in Wonderland — Lewis Carroll
The Canterbury Tales — Geoffrey Chaucer
Heart of Darkness and Other Tales — Joseph Conrad
Robinson Crusoe — Daniel Defoe
A Christmas Carol and Other Holiday Tales — Charles Dickens
Great Expectations — Charles Dickens
Oliver Twist — Charles Dickens
A Tale of Two Cities — Charles Dickens
The Waste Land and Other Writings — T. S. Eliot
A Passage to India — E. M. Forster
The Jungle Books — Rudyard Kipling
Paradise Lost and *Paradise Regained* — John Milton
The Sonnets and Other Love Poems — William Shakespeare
Three Romantic Tragedies — William Shakespeare
Frankenstein — Mary Shelley
Dr. Jekyll and Mr. Hyde and Other Strange Tales — Robert Louis Stevenson
Kidnapped — Robert Louis Stevenson
Treasure Island — Robert Louis Stevenson
Dracula — Bram Stoker
Gulliver's Travels — Jonathan Swift
The Time Machine and *The War of the Worlds* — H. G. Wells
The Picture of Dorian Gray — Oscar Wilde

ANTHOLOGIES

Four Centuries of Great Love Poems

The text of this book is set in 11 point Goudy Old Style, designed by American printer and typographer Frederic W. Goudy (1865–1947).

The archival-quality, natural paper is composed of recyclable products made from wood grown in sustainable forests; the manufacturing processes conform to the environmental regulations of the country of origin.

The finished volume demonstrates the convergence of Old-World craftsmanship and modern technology that exemplifies books manufactured by Edwards Brothers, Inc. Established in 1893, the family-owned business is a well-respected leader in book manufacturing, recognized the world over for quality and attention to detail.

In addition, Ann Arbor Media Group's editorial and design services provide full-service book publication to business partners.